"As our marriages and our homes disintegrate, we often knowingly point our finger at others to assign blame. It is refreshing to read *Is There a Moose in Your Marriage?* which is focused on our own responsibility to be who God has called us to be. Three cheers for Nancy Cobb and Connie Grigsby! Their book gives more than just answers; it gives truth and hope. It is a book that I look forward to sharing with my own daughters."

ANNE GRAHAM LOTZ

*Is There a Moose in Your Marriage?* is a 'must' book for every pastor's library. Nancy and Connie's sound Biblical teaching and Spirit-filled insights can benefit every pastor engaged in premarital and marriage counseling."

REVEREND KENNETH LETTERMAN,
FAITH PRESBYTERIAN CHURCH,
GERMANTOWN, TENNESSEE

"But what gives this book credibility is the transformed marriages in our church because of these author's lives, teaching, and mentoring. This is 'must' reading for women who long for a more fulfilling marriage."

PASTOR WENDELL NELSON

"I am the recipient and blessed husband of a wife who applied (and still does) the principles enumerated in this excellent and very practical book. They have marvelously changed my life on this earth and for eternity."

LARRY WRIGHT, FOUNDER, ABUNDANT LIFE, INC.

"Practical, fun, and absolutely life-changing. You'll laugh, but you will also be inspired. It's perfect for newlyweds but also for those, like me, who have been married a long time and have wonderful marriages. I can't recommend this manual for wives from Nancy Cobb and Connie Grigsby highly enough."

DEE BRESTIN, AUTHOR AND SPEAKER

"Get out your highlighter and read this book...you won't be disappointed!"

KENT JULIAN, DIRECTOR OF YOUTH MINISTRIES

"As a result of the Wife Class (based on material in this book), the women of our church have a clear understanding of God's design for them in their role as wives. As they begin to live accordingly, they reap the benefits of personal peace and new harmony in their marriages."

SENIOR PASTOR ROBERT L. THUNE,
COMMUNITY CHURCH FOR THE CHRISTIAN AND MISSIONARY ALLIANCE,
OMAHA, NEBRASKA

# Is There A MOOSE In Your Marriage?

## NANCY COBB CONNIE GRIGSBY

Multnomah Publishers® *Sisters, Oregon*

IS THERE A MOOSE IN YOUR MARRIAGE?
published by Multnomah Publishers, Inc.

© 2000 Nancy Cobb and Connie Grigsby
International Standard Book Number: 1-57673-635-0

Definitions taken from *Merriam Webster's Collegiate Dictionary,*
Tenth Edition,
Springfield, Massachusetts: Merriam Webster Incorporated, 1994.
Scripture quotations are from:
*The Holy Bible,* New International Version (NIV)
© 1973, 1978, 1984 by International Bible Society,
used by permission of Zondervan Publishing House. All rights reserved.
Also quoted:
*The Holy Bible,* King James Version (KJV)
*New American Standard Bible* (NASB) 1960, 1977, 1995
by the Lockman Foundation. Used by permission.
*The Message*
© 1993 by Eugene H. Peterson
*The Living Bible* (TLB)
©1971. Used by permission of Tyndale House Publishers, Inc.
All rights reserved.
*The Amplified Bible* (AMP)
© 1965, 1987 by Zondervan Publishing House.
*The Amplified New Testament* (AMP) © 1958, 1987
by the Lockman Foundation.

Multnomah is a trademark of Multnomah Publishers, Inc.,
and is registered in the U.S. Patent and Trademark Office.
The colophon is a trademark of Multnomah Publishers, Inc.

For information:
Multnomah Publishers, Inc. • P.O. Box 1720 • Sisters, OR 97759

00 01 02 03 04 — 9 8 7 6 5 4 3 2 1 0

To Ray,
after forty years,
the walk grows sweeter still.

To Dad,
for always showing me the
importance of loving others.
Thank you for the lesson and your love.

To Anne Graham Lotz,
my dear friend and mentor,
who almost twenty years ago
introduced me to
my Savior.

—NANCY COBB

To Wes,
for your commitment,
your integrity,
and your love.

And to Daddy and Mom,
I wouldn't trade my
childhood for
anything in this world.
Thank you.

—CONNIE GRIGSBY

# ACKNOWLEDGMENTS

Thank you to Ed Condra, who from across the ocean in Papua New Guinea, answered our many questions and provided invaluable insight into the Word. Welcome back to the U.S.A., Ed!

Thank you to those who so graciously allowed us to use their stories in this book. Your "realness" adds a dimension that would not be there otherwise. Thanks for sharing. You continue to be a blessing to us.

Thank you to Nancy Thompson, our wonderful editor in Chicago, who became a trusted friend through the editing process. Thanks for polishing our rough edges, spurring us to higher thinking, and warmly encouraging us along the way. Your faith and commitment, especially in the midst of difficult times, is a testimony to God's grace.

Thank you to Multnomah Publishers for giving two first-time authors the thrill of writing their first book. We have thoroughly enjoyed being a part of your team.

Thanks to Bill Alford Jr., who from the sidelines of a sixth-grade basketball game helped affirm the title of this book. We appreciate your enthusiasm and fresh approach.

Thank you to our families and friends for your encouragement and unwavering belief that we should write this book. Thank you for your prayers, your cheers, and your love. The finish line was sweeter because of you.

Most of all, thanks be to God. We love you, Lord, and give You all the glory, honor, and praise.

# CONTENTS

# *Preface*

It was the dead of winter and the temperature was forty below zero. My husband and I (Connie) were living in a remote area of Alaska, and I was traveling along a narrow road one evening, on my way to a friend's home. Suddenly, the vague shape of a rather large object appeared in the road. The closer I got, the larger and more distinct it became. It was a moose! And it was huge.

In fact, the moose blocked the entire road, and I was forced to come to a stop. I honked my horn, shouted, revved my engine, and edged as close as I dared. The moose just stood there, calmly looking at me as if to suggest he wouldn't be the one moving. I had only a couple of options: Go around the moose or go back home.

Just that week someone had frozen to death when his car had broken down and he had left his vehicle to go for help. So going around the moose and risking getting stuck in the snow wasn't an attractive option. So I carefully turned my car around and went back home.

Until I came upon the moose, my journey had gone smoothly. But once a moose got in the middle of it, my forward progress was stopped.

This happens in marriage as well. The union starts off with great hope and anticipation, but then something happens that causes a woman to get off track. She sets her jaw, digs in her heels, and waits on her husband to change before moving forward herself. These kinds of roadblocks that get you off course are what we refer to as "the moose."

There is a collective sigh being heard around the world regarding marriage today. These sighs are being heard within the church as well as outside of it. Disillusioned Christian women are searching for ways around the roadblocks they run up against in their marriages, but the answers seem elusive.

*Or are they?*

It is our belief that they are not. We believe that the answers are presented with clarity in God's Word.

You will see that your role of wife is a holy calling, and that the "how to's" are given clearly in Scripture. You will also discover that as you carry out your responsibilities in marriage, your relationship with Jesus Christ will deepen.

Our purpose for writing this book is simple and heartfelt. We see the tremendous impact these principles have on our own marriages and on the lives and marriages of countless women. We desire the same for you. We pray that through God's grace you will also be challenged and equipped to be an excellent wife. Ultimately, though, our aim is far greater: it's about opening wide the door to knowing God.

Is there a moose in your marriage? Don't let anything impede your forward motion a minute longer. Allow the power of God's Word to get you back on track in your marriage and in your life.

May God richly bless you as you begin to walk down this exciting path.

NANCY COBB AND CONNIE GRIGSBY
OMAHA, NEBRASKA
JUNE 2000

# Part 1

# A Wife's Role

Do you have the aptitude, the capacity, for learning how to become a godly wife? Of course you do! Have you ever wished that there were some kind of job description telling you just how to do this? There is! It was given long ago in a garden called Eden to a woman named Eve. It is a much discussed passage in Scripture and very relevant today.

God's plan is far different from the world's.

*It is harder. It is higher. It is holier.*

His plan for marriage isn't hard. It is impossible! You can never be successful on your own. But the impossible becomes possible because of Jesus. He alone gives us the power to be who He designed us to be—godly women and wives.

Can you do it? Of course! All that's required is your willingness to follow Him.

*Look to Christ...and let the changes begin in you.*

# Given
# by God

*The turning point in a marriage is often so
small and unheralded you can almost miss it.*

**t**here it was. The suitcase. Standing at the top of the basement stairs. The very sight of it made her angry. Her husband had just returned from a business trip and had left the suitcase there, assuring her that very soon he would take it downstairs and put it away.

A week later the suitcase was still there. Since the washing machine was in the basement, she was forced to step over it time and time again as she did the laundry. Before long, the way she treated her husband was directly related to the number of times she stepped over the suitcase. It was the middle of January, and outside the temperatures were dropping rapidly. Inside they were plummeting as well.

One day she decided to move the suitcase. No, she didn't take it downstairs and put it away. Helping was the last thing on her mind. Instead, she carried it into their bedroom and put it down in the middle of the floor where her husband walked, effectively blocking his path to the bed. Now he would see firsthand how irritating it was to arrange one's life around a misplaced suitcase.

She returned to the kitchen expecting to feel a certain amount of satisfaction and relief. She felt neither. Nor did she feel the least bit smug. What she felt was an overwhelming sense of sadness and grief. She knew her husband had not intentionally left the suitcase out; he had simply forgotten about it. Yet even knowing that, she clung to her "right" to feel offended and hostile.

She stood in the kitchen and thought about the suitcase. Had it belonged to guests, she would have happily taken it from their hands and insisted on putting it away herself. So why, she wondered, was she unwilling to help her husband in the same way? Why was it so much easier to serve others than it was to serve her husband? She took a good long look at herself and didn't like what she saw. No wonder she felt grieved. Something needed to change, all right, and it had nothing at all to do with a suitcase.

## A WIFE'S CALLING IS FROM GOD

If someone asked you what the most satisfying aspect of your life is, what would you answer? Is it being a:

Mother?

    Teacher?

        Friend?

            Career woman?

                Grandparent?

Where would being a wife fit? Would it make the top five, or would it fall miserably towards the bottom?

For many years, our marriage relationships were the least fulfilling, least satisfying, and least successful relationships that either of us experienced. Though we didn't know each other at the time, our lives were amazingly similar in this regard. We got along well with everyone else in our lives—our families, friends, neighbors, the postman, the bank tellers, the store clerks. Everyone—except our husbands. This was troublesome and discouraging, but at some point along the way, we let ourselves off the hook by deciding that this surely must be "their problem."

But it wasn't; it was ours. We had no idea what *God's* job description was for us as wives, and so we weren't doing what we could to be the kind of wives God wanted us to be. It was only when we discovered what this job description was and began applying biblical principles to our marriages that we began to find satisfaction and happiness as wives *and* as women.

God never intended for us to be frustrated or confused. He was clear and exact about our role when He stood in His freshly formed garden. *And He hasn't changed His mind.* Popular opinion would have us believe that as the world progresses, so should our thinking. But that is simply not true in regard to God's Word. It remains the one steady thing in a constantly changing world.

## GOD KNOWS OUR DIFFERENCES

In testing the market for this book, we went into a large, nationally known bookstore and asked the manager what books were available on a wife's job description.

"After scanning five hundred entries, all I can find on 'wife' is listed under 'fiction,'" she said.

We told her of our plans to write such a book, and a doubtful expression quickly crossed her face. As we left the store, she called out, "Be careful!"

We asked her what she meant.

"Every woman is so different, how can you possibly write one job description that would fit all women?" she responded.

Of course God knew just how different we are when He specifically spelled out His own expectations, promises, and blessings for a woman who would take on the role of wife as He created it. Just as His Word does not change in a changing world, it does not vacillate according to our differences.

There are three main points that will be discussed in this chapter.

The Role: Helper
The Reason: Man's Aloneness
The Relationship: Marriage

As we look at these aspects of our job description, we will see that they are perfectly designed for us by God.

## THE ROLE: HELPER

God's plan for us was revealed as He put the finishing touches on His creation. It's found in Genesis 2 and is simple and straightforward:

> "It is not good (sufficient, satisfactory) that the man should be alone; I will make him a helper meet (suitable, adapted, complementary) for him. (Genesis 2:18, AMP, emphasis added)

There it is, God's perfect plan for a wife! To be a helper. God's role for a wife in the Garden of Eden is the same one for a wife today. Why would God create and bless all He had brought into being, from the skies and seas to the plants and trees, comment that "It is good," and then deliberately shortchange women? *He would not, and He did not.* We were called by God to a role that only we could fulfill. In God's eyes, creation was not complete without woman.

### And God Created Woman

God had created the heavens and the earth and all things which existed therein and declared them to be not only good, but *very* good. Then God formed man of dust from the ground and breathed life into his nostrils, and Adam became a living being. God gave Adam the responsibility of rulership and cultivating the Garden. He was given the freedom to eat from any tree but one. God warned him that if he did eat from the forbidden tree, he would die (Genesis 1:26–31; 2:7–8, 16–17).

Then God said that it was not good for man to be alone (Genesis 2:18). Adam's *aloneness* was deemed to be "not good" by a

21

perfect God. Have you ever thought about that? This was the first time He said that something about His creation wasn't good.

He had Adam uncover his own need by first directing him to give names to all of the animals. In doing so, Adam discovered that there was no one suitable for him (Genesis 2:19–20). Woman was then created: "I will make him a helper," God said (Genesis 2:18). It is a surprise to many to learn that this role was given while the world was still in its perfect state—*before* sin entered it.

The Lord God caused a deep sleep to fall upon Adam, and as he slept, God took a rib from him and fashioned Eve. God then brought Eve to Adam. When Adam saw her he said, "She is bone of my bones and flesh of my flesh" (Genesis 2:21–23). In effect he was saying, "I am complete when I am with her."

### A High and Holy Title

How does it make you feel to know that you are called to be a helper to your husband? Do you like it? Or do you wish it were different?

We seem to love the idea of God tossing out the stars and calling each of them by name (Psalm 147:4). We are speechless at the very thought of Him, God Almighty, knitting us together in our mothers' wombs and ordaining all of our days (Psalm 139: 13–16). We are awed when we read that He measured the waters in the hollow of His hand and marked off the heavens by His hand's breadth (Isaiah 40:12). These things only confirm to us what we already know—He is God. Awesome, almighty, and perfect. Yet we tend to balk at our role as helper.

In fact, this role is a reflection of who God is.

## A Precious Name

Helper is a title God uses of Himself over and over again in Scripture. The term *helper* is a precious word. There is nothing inferior, demeaning, or second-rate about it.

*Helper is a title God uses of Himself over and over again in Scripture.*

So do not fear, for I am with you; do not be dismayed, for I am your God. I will strengthen you and help you. (Isaiah 41:10, NIV).

God is reassuring His people, telling them not to worry or fear because He, the God of the universe, will be their *helper*.

A friend told us, "Never once have I thought about being a helper in this way. I thought of it as one of the many things I do. But now I see it as who I am. I no longer see it as *doing* something. I see it as *being* someone. I realize that I've never given it the priority that it was meant to have because I was never taught to do so. If Jesus considers being a helper a worthy calling (Hebrews 13:1), then I want to aspire to that calling as well."

This woman had grabbed hold of what being a helper is all about. It's not something you do after you've done everything else. It's not about what you do at all. It's about who you are.

*Helper:* One who gives assistance or support to another, making life more pleasant or bearable.

Would your husband say that because of you, his life is more pleasant and bearable? Would he say he can depend on you for assistance? For support? Or does he shy away from making even the most simple request, fearing your reaction? Mine (Connie's) did.

## A Stubborn Heart

When I (Connie) first heard this teaching, I thought to myself, *You must be kidding. Are you sure about this? God's will for me in my marriage is to be a helper to my husband? And that's all? Simply a helper. Only a helper?*

The verse had a familiar ring to it, yet there was little doubt in my mind that the words, "helper to her husband," weren't meant to stand alone. There must be another phrase qualifying those words. There had to be more to that verse than just that verse!

When I got home I looked at this verse in other versions of the Bible. They all said the same thing. I was thinking, *Why has no one brought this to my attention before? And why now?*

Little did I realize that I was rapidly approaching the turning point in my marriage.

I was less than excited about the idea at the time, however. If being a helper was what it was all about, I'd far sooner *have* a helper than be one. *What a compromise,* I thought, *and what a misuse of the abilities God has given me.* I didn't understand what there was to be excited about. If all of the titles in the world were listed on a sheet of paper, and we could choose just one, I frankly didn't see that there would be a mad scramble for the title of helper.

In the early years of my marriage, however, I actually had been a devoted helper to my husband. Not because I was focused on God's Word, but because of my deep love for my husband. I delighted in making him happy, and I looked for opportunities to lighten his load. Somewhere along the way, though, I got tired of helping. My enthusiasm faded, and I no longer enjoyed doing this. My delight was no longer found in making him happy, and soon I began to keep score.

*Surely,* I thought, *it is time for my husband to do his part. I've done my share, now he can do his.*

My plan was quite simple. I would just slip my heart into neutral until my husband caught on. He didn't catch on very quickly. *This could take longer than I expected,* I said to myself. I dug my heels in a little further, determined to wait him out.

And so began the long siege of waiting for my husband to change. My heart no longer felt like it was in neutral. It was definitely in reverse, and the engine was cold. The young wife who had taken pleasure in tending to her husband's needs was a distant memory. Over time, my heart grew hard. And harder. And harder still.

Things were not working out the way I had envisioned. I shouldn't have been surprised. I was trying to rewrite God's job description to benefit myself. I discovered that neither our hearts nor our wills are able to slip into neutral. They go one way or the other. We are either obeying God, or we are disobeying. At best, using the word *neutral* was an attempt to cloak my disobedience.

When I learned more about God's job description for me as a wife, my heart was stirred. I believe it was the Holy Spirit convicting me of my need to change. It was a humbling time as I considered stepping back into being a wife *God's* way. I found myself taking small steps, even half steps. I was still uncertain, perhaps because of my lack of knowledge, lack of trust, or not wanting to be the one to change. Probably it was a blend of all three. But my way obviously wasn't working. So I confessed:

my pride,

      my disobedience,

            my contentiousness,

                  and my scorekeeping.

I told God that, shaky and unsure as I was, I was willing to do things His way. With a prayer in my heart, I began to reclaim the calling that God had given me. I set out, wobbly legs and all, to be a helper to my husband. Once I chose to do that, I began to feel a joy and a peace that I had not felt for a very long time. I began to experience a deeper relationship with my husband and with my Lord as well.

*How About You?*

If you have been resisting God's Word, what is your reason? Could it be pride? Or bitterness? Or an unforgiving spirit towards your husband? In my case (Nancy), it was ignorance.

I feel that I've had two lives in my marriage. For the first twenty-three years I was busy being a wife in whatever manner suited me for the day. I let my emotions rule my behavior. I didn't know God as He reveals Himself in Scripture—I didn't own a Bible until I was forty-one. I certainly had no idea that He had a plan for me as a wife. For the past seventeen years, however, after discovering what God's Word has to say about marriage, I began to practice the principles in this book in my marriage, and with His help, I have changed.

## THE REASON: MAN'S ALONENESS

It was when the Lord God looked upon the *aloneness* of Adam that He created Eve.

"It is not good (sufficient, satisfactory) that the man should be *alone*. I will make him a helper meet (suitable, adapted, complementary) for him." (Genesis 2:18, AMP, emphasis added)

In researching this book, we asked a male friend to ask his Bible study group this question: "If there is one thing I miss in my marriage it is _____." One of the most frequent answers was *companionship*. Men desire companionship with their mates. They long for someone with whom they can share life's experiences. The men's personality traits, income level, and education had nothing to do with their answers. Companionship was listed by almost every man in the group.

As our friend told us later, "I believe that men are lonelier today than they have ever been. With all of the electronics, video games, reading material, sports programs, and endless list of things you can do to fill up your time, most men have never felt so alone."

Men are lonely today, just as Adam was in the Garden of Eden. Because of this aloneness, woman was created. *Could it be that man's loneliness today may be due in part because women have abandoned their God-given roles and are busy doing their own thing and going their own way?* Has this contributed to man regressing back to the lonely state he knew in the Garden? The question, "Would your husband say he feels less alone because you are his wife?" haunted me (Connie). I remember physically cringing as I contemplated this thought. *Maybe it's not as bad as I think,* I told myself. So I asked my husband about it.

He replied, "I've felt alone many times in our marriage. I remember a point when I felt more alone when I was with you than I did when I was actually by myself. I have never felt more alone than I did at those times."

This was not the reassuring answer I had hoped to hear, yet it came as no surprise. There was a time in our marriage when we both felt that way. There was no talking, no touching, no shared glances, and no laughter.

It is a testimony to God's faithfulness and love that this has changed. This occurred when I began to work on my marriage and apply biblical principles. My heart began to soften, and I saw my husband in a completely different light.

### Putting Words into Action

What can a woman do to make sure her husband isn't lonely? Simply being there for your husband is a wonderful way to begin! One way to be there for him is to show how important he is to you by your attentiveness. How others respond to us shapes the way we see ourselves. Men thrive on positive responses—from their bosses, their coworkers, their customers, but especially from their wives. Is your husband thriving, or is he barely eking out an existence in your home?

I (Connie) had a grandmother whose eyes lit up every time she saw me. She didn't have to utter a single word for me to feel welcome. I could see the sparkle that radiated from those hazel eyes whenever she looked at me. It didn't matter if I was dressed for church or if I'd just come in from making mud pies in her backyard, I felt special every time we were together. She lived on a meager income and left next-to-nothing financially when she died. But she left me with something that no amount of money can buy—the knowledge that I was of great worth to her.

Do you show your husband that he matters greatly to you? Does he feel special in your presence? It is easy to get caught up in

*When your husband is feeling uncertain or worried, can he look at you and feel encouraged?*

the busyness of life and push him farther and farther down on your list of priorities. It may seem that he doesn't notice or that he doesn't mind. But he does.

Does your face soften when you look at your husband? Does your countenance become brighter when he enters the room? Do your eyes convey warmth, or do they send him a message that says he's a long way from where you think he should be as a man, a father, a provider? When he is feeling uncertain or worried, can he look at you and feel encouraged?

What would happen if you began to notice your husband again? If you let him know that you no longer want him to feel alone?

An easy way to get started with this is by something we call "blast-off" and "reentry." It is one of the most effective and powerful things you can do for your husband.

### Blast-off

What are mornings like in your home? Just as there are two critical periods in the voyage of a spacecraft—blast-off and reentry—there are also two critical periods in your home each day. The first is called "blast-off."

Blast-off is our term for when your husband and you say goodbye to each other in the morning. There are probably a dozen other things going on in your home as he, and often you, are trying to get out the door. This is especially true if you have young children.

Mornings are the perfect time to make your husband feel he is not alone. You may be thinking there is not time for one more thing in your schedule. Make time! The few minutes you spend personally sending him off will be one of the best investments you can make in your day—and his.

In chapter 5 we'll go into detail about practical things you can do to control your time; but for now, here are a few tips that will help you create more time in the morning and put the "good" back in "good morning."

- Go to bed at a reasonable hour. If you have young children and haven't established a set bedtime for them, do it now. It may be a battle at first, but it is a battle worth fighting, and everyone will benefit once a routine is established.
- Set your snooze alarm to give yourself five to ten minutes of extra wake-up time.
- Get up fifteen to thirty minutes before your household for a quiet time with God. Pray for your husband and your marriage during this time.
- Take some juice or coffee to him as he's waking up or as he's getting ready for work. You'll be surprised at how much this small effort is appreciated.
- Kiss him, hug him, perhaps say something like, "Welcome to your morning," "Good morning," or "I love you." Your attempts may be awkward at first, but you will be amazed at how quickly the awkwardness goes away and a sense of closeness occurs.
- If you can, fix him breakfast. You might set out a pretty tray

the night before. Put the dishes, glasses, and silverware on it. In the morning, arrange his cereal, fruit, juice, vitamins, and whatever else he needs. If you have fresh flowers in the yard, include them occasionally. This entire process takes only about three minutes! It's well worth the effort, and it makes many men feel loved and special. You need to adapt these suggestions to fit your circumstances, however. One young bride did this for her new husband. After three weeks, he confided that he wasn't a breakfast man and not a morning talker. So she avoided both, much to his delight.

- If you can do only one thing, when he leaves (or before you do) go to him, look in his eyes, and smile. Give him a loving hug and a kiss. Tell him that you love him and that you hope he has a wonderful day. The tone of your voice should be warm and sincere. It may have been a long time since you've done this, and you may feel awkward at first. Don't worry: before long it will seem like you've always done it this way.

As a side note, statistics have shown that a successful blast-off is a safeguard against accidents on the way to work.

### Reentry

Reentry is the second critical time in your home. This is when you and your husband reunite at the end of the day. The first five minutes that you are together set the tone for the rest of the night.

In the comic strip "Drabble," Ralph, the husband/father, is pictured coming home from work. He is met at the door by his wife, who says, "Ralph, that faucet you fixed in the upstairs bathroom is still leaking." Then his two younger children greet him with complaints, "Daddy, Patrick's been calling me a fenderhead!" "Have not!" Patrick retorts. Next, his teenager confesses, "Dad, I inadvertently parked in a tow-away zone today. Can I borrow $160?" In the last scene, Ralph is staring into his bathroom mirror, talking to his image. "Welcome home, Ralph. Good to see you. How are you doing? Fine. Thanks for asking!"

Is this typical of reentry in your home? Do you look forward to your husband coming home each evening, or do you inwardly sigh and think to yourself, "Is he home already?" It is a sad statement if the dog is the only member of the welcoming committee. If your husband gets home before you, find him! Let him know how happy you are to be back with him. Maybe you don't feel happy. You can still greet him with kindness and welcome him home.

Here are some tips to help you with the task of "reentry."

- Pray for a warm, loving reunion.
- If you're home first, watch for his return, and if possible, walk out to meet him as he gets out of the car. This shows that you actually anticipate his arrival.
- Greet him with warmth and affection. Make it a priority to be the first one to greet him each evening.
- Give him a few minutes to unwind. Men frequently say they need time to "deprogram" after working all day. You may be thinking that you'd like a few minutes to deprogram, too, because you've worked all day as well—either in or out of the home—or both! Ask the Lord to help you find the time to do that prior to your reunion. It's amazing how refreshing just a few minutes to yourself can be.

- If your husband is a talker, stop what you're doing and talk with him about his day. If he's the nonverbal type, don't press him for details.
- Don't tell him everything that's gone wrong during the day the minute he steps through the door.
- If your husband enjoys the newspaper when he gets home, don't begrudge his reading it. If he asks you if you've seen a certain article in the newspaper, don't be tempted to tell him that you've been too busy to sit down all day, let alone look at the paper. This kind of self-pity is no fun for him, you, or anyone else within hearing.
- Make it your goal each evening to create an atmosphere that you and your husband enjoy.

### Successful Launches

Two women we know decided to try this idea of "blast-off" and "reentry." The first woman said:

> I was afraid my husband would fall into a coma if I tried this, so I decided to start slowly. When he left in the morning, I simply said, "good-bye," which was a big change from totally ignoring his departure. A few days later I added, "I hope you have a good day." Though that sounds simple enough, it had been so long since I had wished him a good day that it was difficult for me. Next, I began walking my husband part of the way to the door. Then all of the way. I began to wave to him from the window as he left. Over time, I began to watch for him when he came home. I'd start waving at him when he pulled into the driveway.

*One day he waved back!* Before long, I found myself going out to the car to meet him and ask how his day had gone.

To my astonishment, he began to tell me. Not much at first, but over time he told more and more. He has never said anything about the change that has taken place, but I know he notices. Our home is a much happier place.

Said the second woman:

If you had told me this could make such a difference, I would have laughed out loud. But I was desperate and decided to try. Truthfully, my heart wasn't in it, and I wondered why I should be the one doing the work. I didn't feel my husband deserved it. He's usually irritable in the mornings because he's tired and irritable in the evenings because he's tired.

*Why bother?* I thought to myself. I work as well, and I saw this as just one more thing to do before getting out of the house and on my way. Still, I began. Our paths had rarely crossed in the mornings prior to this as we were both getting ready for the day. I think I made him nervous. I was nervous, too.

But I continued on. Though change came slowly, when it did occur it brought with it a long-lost feeling of peace and of knowing that what I was doing was right. Over time, this small thing changed both of us. God used my willingness to minister to my husband to soften my heart. My husband noticed, and *his heart changed as well.* Now it's such a normal part of our day that not doing it would seem strange.

## Begin Today

Women have shared with us that "blast-off" and "reentry" are two of the easiest ways to begin effecting changes in their homes. What's it like in your home? Are your morning departures for work and arrivals back home smooth? Or are they more of the crash and burn variety? Is it time for change? *What would happen if the change started with you?* This is a wonderful, nonthreatening way to introduce genuine warmth back into your home. And there's no better time to start than today!

## God Helps Us Change

If you're seeing that you've made some poor choices in your marriage, don't feel overwhelmed, discouraged, or alone. Praise God that He is stirring your heart to address some of these things now.

Are you willing to do what you can to show your husband that he is not alone? Would you consider moving into the role God created for you? Your answer may be no right now. *Are you willing to be made willing?* Maybe your prayer should be, "Lord, please help me be willing to be willing."

If you feel God tugging on your heart in this area, set about today to make things right. Whether you've been married for a few months or for many decades, it is never too late to begin showing your husband how much he means to you and what a privilege it is to be his wife.

## THE RELATIONSHIP: MARRIAGE

### The Original Wedding

We have seen that God, not wanting Adam to be alone, fashioned a woman from Adam's rib as he slept:

So the LORD God caused the man to fall into a deep sleep; and while he was sleeping, he took one of the man's ribs and closed up the place with flesh. Then the LORD God made a woman from the rib he had taken out of the man, and he brought her to the man. (Genesis 2:21–22, NIV)

How lovely she must have been. She was created in God's own image! We can almost feel God's personal joy as we read the words, "He brought her to the man."

When did they first catch sight of each another? Who saw whom first? Could it have been Adam, who awakening from his sleep, heard the rustling of footsteps and noticed the lovely gift God had given him?

The first recorded human words were spoken by Adam when he said, "She shall be called Woman because she was taken out of man" (Genesis 2:23, NASB).

Then, the Lord God taught the bride and groom His principles for marriage. They were not only for them, but for all generations to come. Now, as then, marriage is to be a commitment of the heart, the will, and the body.

*Commitment of the Heart*

For this reason a man will leave his father and mother...."
(Genesis 2:24, NASB)

Have you and your husband done that? This is not always easy because you both had close personal involvement relationally and traditionally with your own families.

Man is the one that God singles out regarding this issue, but it certainly applies to both of you. This is one of the hardest, but most necessary things a married couple must do. By "leaving" your mother and father, you put your husband in first place in your heart.

Are you a "Daddy's girl?" Do you value your father's opinion more than you do your husband's? Would you rather spend time with your mother than with your spouse? Your husband can resent this to the point that he no longer seems to care for your parents. Would you choose to give your full allegiance to your husband before any other person?

Don't so cling to your family and their ways that you put a wedge between the two of you. You are to be working towards unity with your husband and building your own marital relationship and traditions.

## Commitment of the Will

"...and shall be joined to his wife." (Genesis 2:24, NASB).

You are to effect a close, loyal, unwavering, permanent relationship with your husband. You are to be faithful to one another until death. This involves *choices*.

Ed Wheat, in his book *Love Life for Every Married Couple*, describes the choices like this:

> When God planted the garden of our nature and caused the flowering, fruiting love to grow there, He set our *will* to tend them as a wise gardener. This operation of the will is agape love. Agape love is plugged into an eternal power

source and it can go on operating when every other kind of love fails. Not only that, it loves no matter what—no matter how unlovable the other person is.[1]

Among the things you might consider doing are:

- Ridding your mind of the words "separation" and "divorce"
- Refusing thoughts of men in your past
- Refusing to be self-centered
- Never getting in touch with an "old flame"
- Not telling others about your husband's faults
- Always being faithful. (Faithfulness is a choice that begins in the mind.)
- Upholding your husband's good name
- Not comparing your husband unfavorably with others

## Commitment of the Body

And they shall become one flesh. And the man and his wife were both naked and were not ashamed. (Genesis 2:24–25, NASB)

Isn't this a wonderfully explicit sexual picture? Sex is God's wedding gift. He created you to relish this aspect of marriage.

God's speaking about sex to Adam and Eve was the first thing they heard together as a couple. He intended for them to love each other. One precious expression of their love would be delighting in each other physically. Perhaps that is why Eve's wedding dress was simply her body.

To deny the physical aspect of your marriage is to diminish one of God's greatest gifts to you and your husband. To withhold yourself from your husband, except by mutual agreement, is destructive and wrong (1 Corinthians 7:4–5, NASB). A lack of physical closeness can greatly affect emotional and spiritual closeness. There is something mysteriously wonderful about the physicalness of marriage and of touching.

When I (Nancy) lie down in bed each night with my husband, it is with deep elation and thanksgiving for him. I often tell him that this is the most wonderful moment of my day—to experience his nearness. I know that many couples who have been married as long as we have sleep in separate rooms. This seems sad to me. There is something special about sleeping side by side, touching. In the coldness of this world, the warmest place you know should be your marriage bed.

## RECONSIDERING YOUR ROLE

We have examined the wife's role, the reason for this role, and the context in which this God-given role can be fulfilled. Are you willing to reconsider your role in your marriage? Are you willing to pick up the role of wife, *God's* way? Are you committed to carrying out this role, regardless of what your husband's response is?

There are no limits to what God can do through a heart that is yielded to Him in obedience and trust. In the following chapters, we will review why we struggle with our helper role, examine two foundational principles that will empower us to fulfill God's will for us as wives, and look at some suggestions about how we can deal practically with this wonderful calling.

God said, "It is not good for man to be alone. I will make a helper suitable for him."

We are called to be that helper.

What a challenge…

What a privilege…

*What a Creator!*

## CHAPTER 1 SUMMARY

1.  The first time that God said something was "not good" was in regard to man being alone in the garden.

2.  A wife's role is to be a helper to her husband.

3.  The title of "helper" is a precious term. It is a title Christ uses of Himself.

4.  The role of helper was given *before* sin entered the world.

5.  According to God, it is not good for man to be alone.

6.  "Blast-off" and "reentry" are two of the most effective things you can do in your marriage.

7.  God can do mighty things through a heart that is yielded to Him.

Choices! Choices! Choices! We start making them as soon as our eyes open in the morning. Should I sleep ten more minutes or get up? What's for breakfast? What should I wear? What will I do today?

Some are inconsequential, but some have consequences that can forever alter your world—because some choices are really veiled temptations. The mother of mankind, Eve, faced one temptation that quickly tripled. She saw the tree was good for food—the lust of the flesh. That it was pleasing to the eyes—the lust of the eyes. And a tree to be desired to make one wise—the pride of life. She chose the forbidden fruit (Genesis 3; 1 John 2:16).

Jesus was tempted in the same three ways. Yet He overcame temptation, saying: "It is written… it is written…it is written…." And the devil left Him (Matthew 4:11).

*Arm yourself and resist temptation. In doing so, you will be blessed!*

# CHAPTER TWO

# Choices

*You are always free to choose your actions,*
*but never free to choose your consequences.*

**I** (Nancy) thought we had just become rich. We were moving to Denver, and my husband's salary had doubled. Within a few months, I had a beautiful home built to my specifications, furniture that coordinated perfectly, and a new sports car. This was near the end of the seventies, the decade of the "me generation," and I was at the front of the line.

However, due to my reckless spending, we were soon in a financial crunch. I wondered how I could have done this to my husband and children. All my husband said to me was, "You're going to have to get a job and help pay down this debt load." So I did.

I still remember one of our daughters calling me at work one day. She had just arrived home from school, and it was her birthday. "I'm going to make my birthday cake now," she told me over the phone. Had I not gotten us into that situation, I would have been able to welcome my daughter home with a hug, her birthday cake already baked. I may have called Denver home, but the state I lived in was depression, and the suburb was guilt.

I, like Eve, had been duped into thinking that this "one little thing" could make me happy. In my case, it was an upscale lifestyle and all that went with it: new home, beautiful furnishings, and a shiny new car sitting in the garage. I somehow thought that these worldly goods would elevate me to a whole new level of life.

But I was wrong. I had been deceived. Satan had gotten me to focus my attention on myself. It was a hard lesson to learn regarding expensive tastes, but God used the pit I had dug to begin my journey to know Him as Savior and Lord.

Two years later I bought my first Bible. Two years after that I became involved in a Bible study and learned that Jesus had paid on the cross for all of my sins. And the following year I learned that, like all of us, I had been born a daughter of Eve.

What does this have to do with our role as wives in marriage today? Understanding what went on in the Garden helps us pinpoint why women resist their own role as well as their husbands' in marriage. It is our belief that women *crave* rulership in marriage. This is a consequences of Eve's choice. Because of Adam and Eve's disobedience, God amended the male and female roles. Eve would thereafter be "ruled" by Adam, which is a far more serious state than being "led" by his loving authority.

Let's take another look at what happened in the Garden in order to see how we can begin to reclaim our high calling as wives and begin to get around the road blocks in our marriages.

## APPLES CAN BE SO APPEALING

The LORD God commanded the man, saying, "From any tree in the Garden you may eat freely; but from the tree of the knowledge of good and evil you shall not eat, for in the day that you eat from it you will surely die." (Genesis 2:16–17, NASB)

Eve was the first person ever to struggle with temptation. The handprints of God must have been fresh upon her when a sly serpent entered her world. This creature was more magnificent and crafty than all of the other animals. The choice that would devastate her life was to eat from an apple that hung from a forbidden tree. That same serpent tempts us today with worldly enticements that run counter to the Word of God.

## DID GOD REALLY SAY

God had given Eve dominion over this very serpent when He authorized her and Adam to rule over every living thing. She could have banished him from her sight, but instead she was open and approachable and allowed him to engage her in conversation. He had an offer, and she was interested. With shrewd deliberation, he questioned her understanding of what God had said:

"Did God really say, 'You must not eat from any tree in the

Garden?'" the serpent asked, wanting her to doubt what she knew to be true (Genesis 3:1 NIV).

What he was really asking was this: *Are you sure, Eve? Are you 100 percent sure? How could this be? It makes no sense. Let me clarify this for you.*

Do you notice that when Satan questioned Eve, he made his question sound very similar to what God had actually said? God had said they could eat from any tree *except one*. Satan asked whether they could eat from *any tree at all*. He was creating confusion regarding God's Word, making Eve think that what God said was not what He really meant. *The difference in God's Word and Satan's version of it is the difference between the truth and a lie.*

Eve, caught off guard, found herself considering the serpent's words. Perhaps she was vulnerable because she had not heard the words from God firsthand. She had not yet been created when God spoke them to Adam. Obviously, though, Adam had told her what God had said, and now the serpent was asking her to consider his view.

Eve responded to him, "We may eat fruit from the trees in the Garden, but God did say, 'You must not eat fruit from the tree that is in the middle of the Garden, and you must not touch it, or you will die'" (Genesis 3:2, NIV).

Eve had already added her own twist to what God had said. He had not mentioned touching the tree; He had said only that they were not to eat from it.

Has Satan engaged you in conversation recently? Have you added your own twist to God's Word? Has he caused you to doubt God? Doubt is an insidious thing. It creeps into your life so slowly and so quietly that you may not even realize that it's there.

My (Connie) family once lived in a house with a small bathroom at the back. Every now and then my oldest sister would get upset with me over something and would begin chasing me. I would run through the house and into the bathroom. Once there, I would hurriedly try to slam the door shut, locking it as I slammed. Most of the time I was successful, but occasionally she would get there in time to get just the toe of her shoe between the door and the frame. I knew it would be mere moments before she'd wedge her arm through the door, and then her shoulder, and then her whole body. She was always delighted when this happened, but I was not.

*The serpent still tries to rework God's Word in our lives. His version is usually easy on our ears. He says what we think we want to hear.*

Satan needs only a crack for doubt to come oozing into your life, and he's delighted when you begin to consider forbidden apples. These might be thoughts of another man or that life would be so much easier if only your husband weren't a part of it. The apple represents many different things in your life, but at its core, it stands for the temptation to disobey God's Word.

## DISTORTING GOD'S WORD

After getting Eve's attention and questioning her, the serpent took the simplicity of God's Word and contradicted it, telling her that she would not surely die as God had said. In fact, he assured her that when she ate from the apple, her eyes would be opened and she would be like God, knowing good and evil.

With bold, contemptible brazenness the serpent offered to correct God's Word. What an absurd thought, but he stopped at nothing to convince Eve to disobey. He was unrelenting in his pursuit of Eve, *as he is with us today.*

The serpent still tries to rework God's Word in our lives. His version is usually easy on our ears. He says what we *think* we want to hear. He may even weave in just enough truth to make us think that what we're doing actually has some spiritual merit, but of course it doesn't!

*The Lie*

The serpent busily wove a web of lies and deceit around Eve. He talked and she listened. The longer she listened, the more confused she became. Bit by bit he lured her. Into his plan. Away from God's plan.

He was saying: "You *can* eat from that tree, Eve. There's no reason to deprive yourself any longer. You won't die! He knows very well that the instant you eat from it you will be like Him—able to distinguish good from evil." Satan tempted Eve with the very thing that caused his own fall—his desire to be like God (Ezekiel 28:2, 12–17).

EVE'S CHOICE

Eve pondered the serpent's words. Was she convinced when the serpent assured her that she could actually be like God? This must have been an amazing thought. Surely the serpent had her full attention now. Who would not want to be like Him? Who wouldn't eat from the tree if that was the end result?

Was her brow furrowed as she thought the matter over? Had she heard correctly? Had Adam? Maybe he had forgotten to pass this part on to her. Did God really mean what He had said?

Eve considered the serpent's words. His interpretation seemed so logical. He spoke so boldly. So confidently. So persuasively. The longer she thought, the more she weakened. Eve made her choice. Did all of creation weep when she sank her teeth into the forbidden fruit?

Eve's fall into sin was a progressive one.

*First:* She listened to the serpent's words.

*Second:* She dialogued with him.

*Third:* She considered his lies.

*Fourth:* She chose to believe them.

*Fifth:* She disobeyed God.

How can you protect yourself against the enemy? One of the best ways is to know for yourself what the Word of God says. Then, when confronted with temptation, you are armed. The Bible calls God's Word the sword of the Spirit (Ephesians 6:17).

We have been told that when treasury agents are trained to recognize counterfeit money, they study the real thing. They become so well acquainted with true currency, that they can quickly spot the false. So it is with us. We should be so familiar with God's Word that we immediately recognize an altered version of it.

Before she acted, Eve should have gone to God for clarification of what had been said, but she didn't. Instead, she permitted Satan to lead her step by slippery step into the quagmire of disobedience.

How do you feel about God's directives for your life? It is not unusual for women today to laugh at them. Tragically, Christian women do this as well. We don't realize that the same crafty serpent who lured Eve, is now luring us. *The route he often uses is dissatisfaction with our roles in marriage,* yet we often remain oblivious or apathetic. *Could it be that we have gone our own way for so long that we no longer recognize our behavior as sinful, but instead see it as normal?*

We have been barraged from every angle with the message that the Bible is no longer applicable for today. Talk shows use biblical truths as fodder for audience ridicule. Radio programs tell us to do whatever it takes, with whomever it takes, to find our happiness for the moment. Tragically, our children take this in and learn the same patterns for their own lives.

## THEN AND NOW

It was a disastrous thing when Eve stopped believing God's Word and bought into the serpent's false promises. With that single bite, Eve introduced disobedience into a perfect world. Her life was about to change dramatically. Her actions would affect every living being from that day forward. Because of this sin, we are still susceptible to Satan's lies today.

Over and over again he whispers persuasively, *"Did God really say?"*

*Did God really say* you are called to be a helper to your husband? What an old-fashioned, outdated plan.

*Did God really say* your husband is to be the leader in your home, when you are so much more gifted?

*Did God really say* you should be a godly wife? Your husband is so far from being a godly husband. What is right or fair about that?

## STANDING BEFORE GOD

After Eve ate from the apple, she passed it to Adam, and he, too, ate from it. In their shame, they tried to hide from God.

After He found them, God asked, "Have you eaten from the tree that I commanded you not to eat from?" (Genesis 3:11, NIV).

What utter shame and horror they must have felt. They had stood face-to-face with temptation and given in, and now they stood face-to-face with God. They both knew they had disobeyed His command. It must have been sheer agony to stand before almighty God, knowing they had chosen their way over His.

Most of us look at Eve and wonder how she could have possibly disobeyed God. The right choice seems so obvious to us. Yet every day we make choices, as Eve did, and too often choose her way. Generally, it's easier to pinpoint sin in another's life than in our own.

We are daughters of Eve, and because of that, we sin. Her sin in the Garden is no greater than the sins we commit every day, yet we tend to dilute our disobedience and justify our actions. Our attitude towards sin has become casual. A missionary friend puts it like this: "We've forgotten how God *hates* sin—how He *despises* it. We've become far too comfortable with it, forgetting that it goes against the very character of God. As a result, we allow it greater and greater entrance into our lives, sometimes without as much as a second glance."

Frequently when we do stop and consider sin in our lives, we have a tendency to point the finger at someone else, as Adam and Eve did.

## THE CHAIN OF BLAMING OTHERS

God's question to Adam and Eve was quite simple: had they eaten from the tree or not? Their answers, however, were far from simple. They did some artful dodging and creative thinking. We are about to see the first documented case of something we are all too familiar with: blaming others for our own sin.

Being a quick thinker, but apparently struggling with memory loss, Adam said, "The woman *You* put here with me, *she* gave me some fruit from the tree, and I ate it." He not only blamed Eve, but also God, for giving him the woman in the first place. The Lord turned to Eve, and she responded, "The *serpent* deceived me, and I ate" (Genesis 3:13, NIV, emphasis added). And so began the chain of blaming others for our own sin. It continues today.

Do you ever fall into that trap? Whom or what do you blame when you disobey God?

Your husband

Your kids

Your upbringing

Your schedule

Your finances

Stress

Headaches

Heartaches

The only person to blame when you choose disobedience is yourself. Jesus says, "If anyone loves me, he will obey my teaching.... He who does not love me will not obey my teaching" (John 14:23–24, NIV). Do you love Jesus? Do you obey His Word? According to this verse, you can't say yes to one, and no to the other because your love or lack of it is demonstrated by your obedience.

## A WOMAN'S INFLUENCE

The fact that a woman has tremendous influence in a man's life was dramatically proven when Eve passed the apple to Adam, and he ate from it. God had spoken *directly* to him and told him not to eat from it. Yet in the presence of Eve, his resolve softened, and he chose to disobey God. It is impossible to overstate the incredible influence Eve had in his life.

We cannot take this principle lightly in our own lives today. We greatly influence our husbands' lives and choices. A woman's ability to get her husband to do what she wants has not weakened since the Garden. She can even do this in the name of godliness. This is such a powerful thing that she must be constantly checking herself to see that this power is not misused.

Do you misuse the influence you have in your husband's life? Do you offer anything to him that is not pleasing to God? Eve did, and because of this, she, along with Adam, faced severe consequences.

## CONSEQUENCES

Sin never visits us alone. It travels with a companion called *consequence*. Every time you sin, there is a consequence. This was seen first in the Garden immediately after Adam and Eve chose to disobey God.

God prefaced Adam's consequences with the words "because you listened to your wife" (Genesis 3:17 NIV). Adam's consequences were a direct result of Eve's influence. Even though Adam had free will and was responsible for his disobedience, Eve's part in this did not go unnoticed. God sees what we do in our husbands' lives! What a motivation this should be to us as wives.

God went on to tell Adam that from then on his labor would be exhausting because of a curse on the ground. Adam had worked before the Fall, but now his work would be toilsome.

### Eve's Role Is Amended by God

Eve's consequences would include greater pain in childbearing, and we're told her desire *and* craving would be for her husband:

> Yet your desire *and* craving will be for your husband, and he
> will rule over you." (Genesis 3:16 AMP)

Certainly there is a deeper meaning here than that a woman would continue to desire her husband sexually. *Crave* means to demand, to want mastery over, to want greatly, to need as one needs drugs. There is nothing passive about this word.

What is it that women crave today perhaps more than anything else? Could it be that what we crave refers to the second part of woman's consequence for her sin? *Is it the desire to rule over our husbands?*

Susan Foh, in her book, *Women and the Word of God: A Response to Biblical Feminism,* explains:

> The "curse" here describes the beginning of the battle of
> the sexes. After the fall, the husband no longer rules easily;

he must fight for his headship. The woman's desire is to control her husband (to usurp his divinely appointed headship), and he must master her, if he can. Sin has corrupted both the willing submission of the wife and the loving headship of the husband. And so, the rule of love founded in paradise is replaced by struggle, tyranny, domination, and manipulation.[1]

Never should Adam have followed Eve's lead. She desired to take the lead from her husband and have him do what she wanted. Now both are condemned. Her punishment matches her sin: man is to rule over her, not simply lead her. Man is punished for submitting to her lead. It is important to remember that this is not a passage about husband and wife relationships as we find in later revelation in the New Testament. This is a passage about consequences—the punishment of mankind for sin.

Before the Fall, there was a positive complementary relationship in which the husband was the leader and the woman the "complementer." Since the Fall, the man *rules*. We see that throughout history that women have been ruled over by men, often cruelly. The New Testament teaches the husband how to rule in this fallen world beyond Eden with *love* for his wife, rather than being tyrannical. He is told to *love* his wife in order to temper the judgment of *rule* over the woman, so it is done in the way that was proper before the Fall.

In the New Testament the woman is asked to *respect* her husband's leadership, the very thing she was trying to supplant when she sinned and which prompted the man to sin.

It appears to us that the New Testament is trying to get man and wife back into a more complementary relationship, one like that which existed prior to the Fall, yet which recognizes the consequences of the Fall.

Undoubtedly, Eve felt hopeless and lost as she realized just how much that bite of apple had cost. Surely she clung to the words God had spoken to the serpent:

> "I will put enmity between you and the woman, And between your seed and her seed; He shall bruise you on the head, And you shall bruise him on the heel." (Genesis 3:15, NASB)

There would be a continuous struggle between opposing forces: Satan's and man's. Yet the seed of woman would deliver the fatal blow to Satan. You and I know who that is. *It is Jesus!* He is the holy offspring of Mary, who conceived Him as the Holy Spirit came upon her.

In His mercy and love, God forced Adam and Eve out of the Garden, blocking their approach to the tree of life. If they had eaten of that tree, they would have stayed perpetually locked in their sin.

Praise God, you and I live on this side of the Cross. Jesus became the curse for us so that we would have eternal life. He came to earth to die on the cross to pay the price for our sins.

*Living on this side of the Cross* simply means that through the blood of Jesus, those who have asked Him to be their Savior have the power to live their lives in a new way, based on the truth of God's Word.

Have you taken that step and accepted Jesus as your Savior? We've outlined the simple steps of how to do so on the next page.

## THE PLAN OF SALVATION

To receive Christ you need to do four things:

1. ADMIT your spiritual need. "I am a sinner."
2. REPENT and be willing to turn from your sin.
3. BELIEVE that Jesus Christ died for you on the cross.
4. RECEIVE, through prayer, Jesus Christ into your heart and life.[2]

This plan is seen in Scripture in the following verses: Romans 3:23; 1 John 1:7–10; John 3:16; and John 1:12.

Romans 10:13 says "Everyone who calls on the name of the Lord will be saved." What might you pray if you wish to do this? Perhaps a prayer like this:

*Dear Jesus,*

*I admit that I am a sinner. I want to turn from my sins. I believe that You died on the cross for me. I ask You to come into my heart and my life as my Lord and Savior. Thank You for dying on the cross for me and for saving me. Amen.*

Once you do this, you are "born again" into the family of God. This is all that is required for entering the kingdom of God (John 3:7).

My (Connie) friends and I used to discuss what being "born again" meant. It wasn't a commonly used term when I was young. I wasn't sure what it meant and even less sure that I needed it. Although I had accepted Christ at an early age, I worried for years that I hadn't done enough to assure that I would go to heaven and be with Him when I died. It was not until adulthood that I learned I had done all that was needed. And so have you, if you have prayed to trust Christ as your Savior. Certainly your spiritual growth will always be in process, but the assurance of salvation is there the instant you receive Christ.

*Jesus wants to be your Savior.* No matter where you've been, what you've done, or what kind of life you're leading currently, He longs for you to ask Him into your heart. His death on the cross covered everything. *There is nothing you've done or can do that isn't covered by His blood, except to reject Him.*

Not long ago, very early in the morning I (Connie) pulled into the parking lot of the hospital where my husband works. It was not yet five o'clock, and the front doors were still locked. As I got out of my car, I noticed a young couple standing at the revolving doors, trying to force them open. The husband was pushing with all his might, but they wouldn't budge. As I got closer, the woman turned toward her husband with a look of desperation on her face. She was near tears. As she turned, I saw that she was nine months pregnant, dressed in her robe, and in hard labor. "The doors are locked and we can't get in," the man cried out to me as I approached. "My wife's in labor. We've got to get inside." He was very young, and his voice cracked with urgency and fear.

I was familiar with the hospital and knew there was a side door just a few steps away that most likely was open. If it wasn't, there was a phone tucked inside a box just inches away, and we could call the security office. With a click of a button, they could unlock the doors.

We tried the side door and it opened. The couple was so relieved. I ran to the elevator and pressed the button for the Ob-Gyn floor, holding the doors open until they came. "Is this your first?" I asked. "Yes!" the young man said, "and we think it's a boy!" I wished them well, and they were gone.

Somewhere out there is a little child whose parents will one day tell him that when they finally got Mom to the hospital, the doors were locked, and they didn't know how to get inside until someone showed them.

The door of heaven is open to you today. Jesus Himself unlocked the door for those who would receive Him by faith. There is no reason to stand outside anymore. The only thing needed for admission is for you to repent of your sins and trust Jesus as your Savior. If you haven't done this, won't you consider doing so now?

If you've just made this decision, or if you are a new Christian, seek out a Bible-teaching church in your area. Ask God to help you find someone who will help you grow in your spiritual walk.

## INTERACTION BASED ON LOVE

Jesus showed us by His life how to live and how to love. No longer do we have to live under the curse; we have the ability to live with freedom (Galatians 5). The power struggle for leadership in the home can be a thing of the past.

There is a new God-given way to be a husband and wife. Our interaction with each other is to be based on love (Ephesians 5:1–2). A husband is to love his wife as Christ loved the Church. A wife is to respect and submit to her husband as to the Lord (Ephesians 5:22, 25). These principles will be discussed more fully in chapter 5.

Because of Jesus, we have available to us a new life, a new nature, and a new freedom. Sin's power over us is broken. We are no longer under its control. We share in Jesus' life. We can consider ourselves to be dead to sin, but alive to God. We have been freed from sin. The penalty for sin and its power over our lives died with Jesus on the cross.

Even though we still feel like sinning and sometimes do, we are no longer slaves to our sinful nature. Now we can choose to live for Christ.

## TIMELESS QUESTIONS

Did you know that the first two questions to appear in the Bible occur when Adam and Eve ate of the apple?

The first question, *Did God really say, "You must not eat from any tree in the garden?"* (Genesis 3:1 NIV) was asked by the serpent. The door by which sin entered the world was this question. Satan's motive in asking this of Eve was to cause her to disobey God. His motive is unchanged as he asks us this same question today.

The second question, *"Where are you?"* (Genesis 3:9 NIV) was asked by God. As He walked through the Garden in the cool of the day, He asked Adam where he was, knowing full well that he and Eve were hiding because of their sin.

Perhaps you could apply this same question in your marriage: *Where are you?* Are you following God's plan for your marriage? Are you bringing honor to God in your role as a wife, or would you, too, be tempted to hide from God?

Don't allow yourself to be taunted by the enemy's words: *Did He really say?* Don't allow his lies to win the battle regarding what you're going to do. Don't permit him to convince you that your husband doesn't deserve a godly wife. *It is the Lord Himself who desires your godliness and obedience.*

We will be giving you many ideas about being a helper to your husband in obedience to your calling as a wife. In the next two chapters we will be examining two areas that are foundational to becoming empowered to be a godly wife. However, just as we have seen in the life of Eve and in our own lives, this involves choices. One of the ways we can learn to *persist* in our efforts to become godly wives is to learn to choose right actions over our feelings.

## ACTION VERSUS FEELING

By and large, many women operate on their feelings. But these very feelings often get a woman off track. If we're upset or irritated with our husbands, it shows in our actions toward them. Or if we think we're doing our part, but feel they're not doing theirs, we shut down. We want to be godly wives—as long as our husbands are treating us as we think they should. Our actions toward our husbands are often determined by whether we feel they deserve such treatment. The minute they step over a certain line, which has been predetermined by us, our efforts stop.

What in the world would happen to a marriage if, through the Holy Spirit's power, a woman chose to act in godly ways, *regardless* of her feelings?

In their book *Happiness is a Choice*, Frank B. Minirth and Paul D. Meier say that it's fine to try to understand our feelings as best we can, but the real focus should not be on our feelings, but on our behavior. They write: "You don't do what you do because you feel the way you feel—you feel the way you feel because you do what you do." They go on to explain, "Think about that for a moment.

In other words, your actions (godly or ungodly) will determine how you feel. If you choose to love your mate, for example, and choose to act lovingly and respectfully toward your mate, the feelings of love will follow whether it was there before or not."[3]

Feelings are natural and normal, but we have little control over them. What we do have control over is our behavior. If we desire to be godly wives, we must carefully, prayerfully choose what our actions will be and let them take priority over what we happen to be feeling at the moment.

## WHO'S DRIVING YOUR CAR?

To paint a clearer picture, think of your feelings and actions as if they were passengers in an automobile. Who is behind the wheel, steering your car? If you're like most women, your *feelings* are doing the driving and your *actions* are in the backseat.

The only thing necessary for your actions to be doing the driving is for you to put them behind the steering wheel. To do this, you will need to remove your feelings from the driver's seat and put them in the backseat.

As you do this, at first your car may careen wildly back and forth across the road—it may have been a while since they have had to do any steering. But don't give up! Your actions may be hesitant to drive the car, and your feelings will be trying to tighten their grip on the wheel because they don't like sitting in the backseat. Keep them there anyway, and train your actions to drive.

As you weather the bumps and curves that you'll encounter, the trip will begin to smooth out, and over time your actions will be driving the car with ease and expertise.

*You don't do what you do because you feel the way you feel—you feel the way you feel because you do what you do.*

Remember one thing though: No matter how loudly your feelings are screaming from the backseat, leave them there. As you allow your actions to navigate where you go, your feelings will begin to follow. Maybe not immediately and maybe not naturally at first, but eventually they will fall into line with your actions.

When I (Connie) heard this teaching, I thought to myself, *How can I possibly act in a way I do not feel?* It sounded impossible, unpleasant, and hypocritical. The thing that bothered me the most, however, was that I didn't think my husband deserved such treatment. But I was tired of:

living in frustration…

making all the rules…

changing all the rules…

being the judge and jury…

having a heart of stone…

being a poor model to my children…

My marital roller coaster seemed to take more and more energy to get to the top of the track. In fact, it had been a very long time since we had been anywhere near the top. What did I have to lose? I humbly asked God to help me:

…Give up my pride

…Stop keeping score

…Soften my stony heart

…Let go of my bitterness

...Put my husband before myself

...Put my husband before my children

...Stop thinking that I always knew best

...Rekindle the love and joy that I once felt

I asked Him to help me start acting the way I wanted to feel and stop being controlled by the feelings that raged within me. With His help, I wrenched my feelings out of the driver's seat and put them into the backseat. Then I cleaned the rust off my rarely used actions and nervously put them behind the wheel of my car. I took a deep breath and stepped out of my comfort zone a little bit. And then a little more. And even more. The car lurched and jerked and sputtered and spewed, but it kept going.

As I write this, tears come to my eyes as I remember how God was there for me—how He held my hand as my shaky legs began to carry me down this unknown path. How He assured me that this was right, when my pride tried to tell me otherwise. And how He encouraged and blessed me as I began to do and say things to my husband that I hadn't said or done in a very long time.

I can't begin to tell you the joy I felt as my heart began to soften. And as it softened, my husband began responding. I no longer had him backed into a corner, daring him to come out. He no longer felt he was walking in a field covered with land mines, never quite knowing when I would erupt. I had finally given him some freedom to be who he was without instant retaliation when he wasn't who I wanted him to be.

My feelings were beginning to catch up with my actions. No one was more surprised than I was. My only regret was that I hadn't chosen to do this sooner.

If you've never chosen actions like this before, will your husband think things are suddenly strange? Will he even notice? Most likely he will. He may even question why you're acting in such a way. But you know! And God knows! You are doing it in your desire to be a godly wife, knowing it brings honor and glory to Jesus Christ.

What better reason is there to begin?

## CHAPTER 2 SUMMARY

1.  Disobedience entered the world when Eve chose to eat from the apple after being tempted by the serpent.

2.  The first question asked in the Bible—when the serpent asked Eve, "Did God really say?"—is still being asked of women today.

3.  As a consequence of Eve's sin, women want the rulership role in their homes and will frequently go to any length to get it.

4.  Hope came through Jesus, who became the curse for us.

5.  By His life, Jesus showed us how to live and love.

6.  Because of Him, we can live on "this side of the Cross."

# Part 2

# Laying the
# Foundation

There is a fragrance that exists today that is far more beautiful than anything you can buy at the cosmetics counter of the nicest store. It is priceless, yet it is freely available to all who desire it: the rich, the poor, the educated, the illiterate—to all ages, races, incomes, professions. It is available to kings and queens, to common thieves, to you and me.

The fragrance is forgiveness—a fragrance so strong it can transform your life. A fragrance so beautiful it can soften bitter hearts. A fragrance so sweet it will cause others to look at you and wonder just what it is that makes you so different.

Forgiveness—something that was freely given on the cross and something we can freely give others. It is life changing, God honoring, and the key to successful relationships.

*Forgiveness—have you accepted His priceless gift?*

# CHAPTER THREE

# Forgiveness

*Forgiveness is the fragrance of the violet
on the heel that crushed it.*——MARK TWAIN

**A** friend of ours recently told us how she and her husband
sat at the dinner table one night and began talking about the important events that had marked their twenty years of marriage. They
spoke of their wedding, their first home, a completed education,
dozens of friends, several moves, and finally, the births of their children.

As they thought back over those times, her husband said that
there was something else that stood out in his mind, perhaps
eclipsing everything that had just been discussed. Our friend had

no idea what it was. Her husband was not one for details and remembered little of past events.

"I remember the evening as if it happened yesterday," he said. "It was the night you told me you no longer held against me the unhappy years in our marriage. You said you forgave me and suggested we bury those sad times and set about building new memories to replace them. I knew I had been hard on you in the past and that the wedge that had developed between us was due largely to that. I knew also that I had never really taken full ownership of the hurt and rejection that resulted, preferring instead to let bygones be bygones. So when you said those words to me, it was as if a huge weight was lifted from my shoulders. I felt free. I felt hopeful. I felt forgiven. I felt alive again, in a way that I had not felt for a very long time."

Our friend was flabbergasted. She had no idea that her words had so profoundly affected him. As he told her later, he felt the course of their marriage was redirected that evening; no longer would the veil of unforgiveness constantly cloud their marriage.

As she reflected, she realized how, almost nonchalantly, she had allowed him to live with the pain and guilt of knowing he had hurt her. In fact, some days she had even encouraged it. Yes, he had been hard on her in their early years, but surely she had retaliated by being hard on him in a far worse way.

"What prompted your seemingly sudden forgiveness?" we asked her.

"I was at a point in my life where I desired an intimate relationship with God—I had kept Him at arm's length for so long. I knew, however, that for this to happen, I would have to deal with my lack of forgiveness. I believe this was the primary hindrance to my having an intimate relationship with God. That was the motivating factor," she said.

"Naively, I thought I was doing my husband a favor by wiping the slate clean. However, I discovered that I was the one who benefited most. No longer did the pall of unforgiveness permeate my heart and home. Our marriage gears began moving forward again. They had been motionless for so long, locked tightly around old hurts from the past. I thought they had come to a grinding halt because of my husband. Looking back, however, I see that it was my lack of forgiveness that prevented our forward growth. When I forgave my husband, we felt as though we were starting over, and in a sense we were. Our marriage was changed and I was changed the day I chose forgiveness."

Are your marriage gears as tightly locked as this woman's were? There is nothing like the oil of forgiveness to get them moving again! It is impossible to overstate the importance of forgiveness in your role as wife. We feel this is one of the most misunderstood, least practiced principles in Scripture. A lack of forgiveness puts roadblocks in your marriage and short-circuits your ability to be a helper to your husband. As you will discover in the pages ahead, forgiveness changes lives and allows you to have a full, vibrant relationship with God.

## THE POWER OF FORGIVENESS

This whole area of forgiveness is a subject that is dear to both of us because we were both unforgivers. We were quick to anger and slow to forgive. We never analyzed it; we just thought "that's the way feelings work." We would wait until we no longer felt angry to forgive our husbands for whatever we were holding against them.

Our feelings dictated our choices. Because of a lack of understanding in this area, we were held hostage by our unforgiveness, even erroneously thinking that at times we had no choice in the matter. We discovered what a ridiculous way this is to live.

Being held hostage is like being chained to a perceived offense. Let me (Nancy) give you an example. Ray and I had been married for six years. We had four children, a small house, and furniture that had seen better days. The only really nice thing I owned was a set of bright red canisters that my sister had given me. Every time I saw them it made me feel special. One day Ray was on the phone and extended the long cord attached to the kitchen wall to its limits, probably to fetch a child. In so doing, he inadvertently caught the lid of one of my canisters, causing it to fall to the floor and break. I was inconsolable. Ray was very sorry and asked me to forgive him. But I couldn't. Isn't that absurd? So I wallowed in my sorrow and distanced myself from him. Of course, this quickly spilled over into our communication—I was chilly, if I even spoke.

I was a hostage to my feelings. I had no idea at the time that I could free myself and my marriage from this situation. It was years before I broke out of this fruitless way of living.

Understanding and applying the magnificent antidote of quick forgiveness is the privilege of a real helper in a marriage. In fact, it is essential to any successful relationship, not just between a husband and wife, but in all other relationships as well. Incidentally, by God's grace, He has given both of our husbands a "supernatural amnesia" about our early years as unforgiving wives.

Learning to forgive our husbands freed us from the shackles of allowing our emotions to take precedence in our marriages. Although difficult at first, we knew we were pleasing God, and that is what kept us going forward when we felt unforgiving. To our surprise, it became easier and easier, although we still had (and have) our days.

Jesus addressed the importance of forgiveness when He instructed the disciples how to pray. After finishing what we know as the Lord's Prayer, He said:

> For if you forgive men when they sin against you, your heavenly Father will also forgive you. But if you do not forgive men their sins, your Father will not forgive your sins. (Matthew 6:14–15, NIV)

Did you notice that the only point in the Lord's Prayer that Jesus emphasized was about forgiveness? Certainly if He is instructing us how to pray, every word is of utmost significance. But it is interesting to note that He addressed forgiveness an additional time.

*A woman will not be a helper to her husband when she is absorbed in recounting others' offenses towards her.*

Next to your own salvation, forgiveness may be the most important issue you will face in your lifetime. As you apply some of the following principles to your life, you will be able to see why you are the way you are and why you keep doing the things you do. You may also gain insight as to why your husband, your children, your parents, or your friends behave as they do. You will learn why your relationship with your husband and others may be so erratic—warm and loving one minute, cold as ice the next.

Are your feelings holding you captive? Are you exhausted from waiting for just the right time to forgive your spouse for whatever it is you're angry about? Don't wait! Life is far too short and your relationships much too important to wait a moment longer.

Understanding the principles of forgiveness will transform your life and the lives of those close to you. The motive for forgiving is simple: Jesus requires it. If we want to be like Him, then we must choose to be forgivers. Let's look at some basic principles that are involved.

## PRINCIPLE 1: FORGIVENESS IS ACCOMPLISHED THROUGH CHRIST'S POWER

The power to forgive comes through Christ. It was His death on the cross that enables us to forgive. Through that act, forgiveness spills out onto everyone who receives Him as Savior. You, in turn, are able to extend this same forgiveness to others.

Not long ago we heard the story of a woman who had experienced severe pain and abuse when she was growing up. As an adult, many years later, she accepted Christ as her Savior. Through tears, she shared how she then was able to forgive those who had hurt her. Previously, although she had tried, she had no power to do this because the source of forgiveness had not been living in her.

Knowing Christ as your Savior is only the beginning to unlocking the doors of forgiveness. Many people can know Him as Savior, yet continue to live their lives locked in the grip of unforgiveness. Such was the case with Carol.

## A Daughter's Heartache

Carol is a woman who appears to have it all. In her thirties, she is tall, slender, attractive, and energetic. She has a handsome and adoring husband, two well-adjusted teenagers, a beautiful home, a great job, extended family support, and she is involved actively in her community. More importantly, she has known the Lord for years.

Few people would guess that Carol struggles with something that causes her great grief and sadness. Over the years it has filled her with a negative, critical spirit that she masterfully covers up whenever she is in the public eye. Outward appearances show a woman who is happy, yet if you knew Carol well, she would tell you that her heart aches almost every day. She longs for true joy and contentment, but thus far they have eluded her. The problem? Carol is an unforgiver. She was raised in a loving, Christian home, but her parents have always favored her brother. Because of this, Carol harbors deep resentment. Both her brother and parents live nearby, so she is faced constantly with the situation.

"I've tried to forgive my parents, but can't seem to do so. Just when I think I have, something else happens, and I'm right back to where I was. They make such an effort to be a part of my brother's life. They drive right past my house on their way to visit him, yet rarely do they stop to see me."

Carol continues, "It was bad enough before he had children because until then they treated all of their grandchildren the same way. Now my brother's children are favored openly. They catered to my brother all of his life and now cater to his children. Their favoritism has extended to another generation. My children notice it—how could they not? It is one thing when they slight me, but it's an entirely different matter when they slight my children."

People close to the family would agree that partiality is shown. One of Carol's siblings overheard two aunts discussing the situation. "They are proud of all their kids," they said, speaking of her parents, "but Mike is their pride *and* joy."

Carol holds unforgiveness in her heart but feels powerless to do anything to change the situation. In her mind, she is the victim of parents who haven't used wise judgment. In reality, it is her unforgiving heart that causes her to *feel* the way she does.

She can change this by choosing to forgive her parents, regardless of whether or not they change. This power was given to her when she accepted Jesus as her Savior, but she can choose whether she will utilize this power or not.

Think of a brand-new, shiny toaster sitting on your counter. Unless you press the lever that causes it to begin toasting, it will not work, even though it is capable of doing so.

Carol is much like that toaster. She has the power to forgive, but isn't activating it. An unforgiving heart is a heavy weight to carry. It will affect everyone around you, especially your husband, for the marriage relationship generally bears the brunt of an unforgiving heart in either partner. A woman will not be a helper to her husband when she is absorbed in recounting others' offenses toward her. Unless you avail yourself of God's power to forgive freely, you'll find yourself hashing out another's offense toward you over and over again. When you don't forgive, the tendency to dwell on things is stronger than the tendency to forgive. You must choose forgiveness in order to get on with your life, and in order to glorify God.

Is this happening in your marriage? Do you find yourself reliving over and over again how another has wronged you? If so, reconcile this issue today. How? Ask God to forgive you for your unforgiving heart. Then choose to forgive that person for his or her offense toward you. Perhaps it would help to talk with a pastor or a godly friend. You'll be amazed to discover how your forgiveness of others clears the way for you to be a helper to your husband in the way God intended.

## PRINCIPLE 2: FORGIVENESS IS LIMITLESS

Do you ever tire of forgiving? Do you feel that you have done more than your fair share in this area? Have you set up a mental checklist of prerequisites that must be met in order for you to offer forgiveness to another? Is there a limit on how many times you are required to forgive another? Jesus answered those questions in a conversation He had with Peter, who was refreshingly honest when he asked Jesus, "Lord, how many times shall I forgive my brother when he sins against me? Up to seven times?" (Matthew 18:21, NIV).

*Don't we also do that as wives?* We forgive our husbands a number of times, but then their forgiveness quotient is used up, and rather than continuing to forgive, we begin keeping a record of their mistakes, forgetting that love doesn't take into account a wrong suffered (1 Corinthians 13:5). We do this with others as well. We draw an imaginary line in the sand, and once that line is crossed, we are through forgiving.

But as we're about to see, this isn't God's way of doing things! Listen to what He says as He instructs Peter in this area:

"I tell you, not seven times, but seventy-seven times." (Matthew 18:22, NIV)

In other words, He says we are to forgive over and over again. *Stop counting and start forgiving.*

Often a wife finds it easier to forgive her husband the first few times he offends than she does after he's done something for the umpteenth time. The husband of a friend of ours has a habit of becoming short-tempered and agitated whenever he's hot or tired. They live in the South, and he has a highly stressful job, so the opportunities for him to be irritable are unlimited! And often he takes full advantage of those opportunities. His behavior is wearying to her, and at times she finds herself reluctant to forgive him one more time for the same irritation. "Why can't he see what he's doing and change?" she wonders. "I've told him often enough." She has discovered, however, that when she withholds forgiveness, she is the one most miserable.

When you don't forgive, you are effectively saying, "I no longer want to be like Christ." *Of course, that is never the place of blessing.* Our passion should be to dwell in that blessed place! For our friend, it is this simple yet powerful thought that spurs her, as it should us, to forgive her husband over and over again.

Many times it is basic personality differences that are the kindling for a raging fire of harsh words, snide remarks, and flippant behavior. In fact these things sometimes happen many times in the course of one day.

In his study guide, *Discover Your Giftedness in Christ,* Dr. Mels Carbonell profiles four models of human behavior based on temperament.[1] My (Nancy) husband is at one end of the scale and tends to be direct, decisive, determined, and driven. I fall towards the other end, and my temperament is almost the direct opposite of my husband's. For a long time I wondered, "Why can't Ray be more like me? Then we'd be *so* happy!" What seemed common sense to me at the time was nothing more than pride on my part.

It was life changing to discover that what I was holding against him was intrinsic to his God-given personality. Before long I realized that what I actually would not forgive was his *personality!*

Look at your own relationship. Is personality type one of the reasons for discord in your marriage? This is a form of lovelessness and reveals a judgmental spirit. A wise woman understands the way her husband is wired and accepts him for who he is. God complements and balances a couple through their differences.

When problems crop up in your marriage, as they continue to in ours, remember that forgiveness is limitless. Choose to honor God by forgiving easily and often.

## PRINCIPLE 3: FORGIVENESS OF OTHERS SHOULD MIRROR GOD'S FORGIVENESS OF YOU

Matthew 18 clearly illustrates this principle. Jesus spoke of a servant who owed a king approximately ten thousand talents, a vast sum of money. The servant was unable to repay the king, so the king ordered that the servant, his wife, his children, and all that he had be sold to repay the debt. Everything that he had, *including his family,* was to be sold in order for the king to be repaid.

But the servant fell on his knees before the king and begged, "Be patient with me, and I will pay back everything."

The king took pity on him, canceled the debt, and let him go. He didn't merely adjust the debt or give the servant more time to come up with the money. He canceled the debt in full.

The forgiven man left and soon came upon a fellow servant

who owed him a hundred denarii, or about a hundred days wages. This was just a pittance compared to what he had owed the king. Yet he grabbed his fellow servant and began choking him. "Pay back what you owe me!" he demanded.

His fellow servant fell to his knees and begged, "Be patient with me, and I will pay you back."

What a perfect opportunity for the servant to follow the king's gracious example by extending that same grace to another. But instead, he refused to forgive the meager debt and had the man thrown into prison until he could repay what he owed. He didn't offer to adjust or cancel the debt, but chose to take swift, harsh action.

When the other servants saw what had happened, they were greatly disturbed and reported to the king everything that had just taken place.

What do you think the king did when he heard the news? It would seem natural that he would rush to the jail and release the imprisoned man. However, that's not what happened. Instead, he called the unforgiving man in for a conference.

Not mincing words, he said, "You wicked servant, I canceled all that debt of yours because you begged me to. Shouldn't you have had mercy on your fellow servant just as I had on you?" In anger, the king turned him over to the jailers to be put in prison *and tortured* until he paid back all he owed.

Did you notice that the unforgiving man was put into prison for nonpayment of debt? *The very thing he wouldn't forgive came back into his own life.*

Jesus tells us that if we pardon and release (give up resentment and let it drop), we will be pardoned and released.

> Do not judge, and you will not be judged. Do not condemn, and you will not be condemned. Forgive, and you will be forgiven. (Luke 6:37, NIV)

In the parable about the unforgiving servant, did you notice that he was put into prison *and tortured?* The unforgiving man was then in the same position as the man he has just refused to forgive, but worse. He was imprisoned *and tortured* until he paid back all that he owed. The huge debt that the king was once willing to cancel was back on him. The "forgotten" debt was remembered, and would not be dropped until payment was made in full. The story ends with a riveting statement.

> This is how my heavenly Father will treat each of you unless you forgive your brother from your heart. (Matthew 18:35, NIV)

Unless we forgive our brothers from our heart! *This passage reveals that unforgiveness actually affects how we will be treated by Christ.*

The city where we live has garbage collection once a week. On one occasion, due to a snowstorm, my (Connie) family didn't get the trash taken to the curb in time to be picked up. By the next week, we had trash spilling everywhere.

When you don't forgive others in a timely manner, your heart begins spilling over with garbage and it's called bitterness. When you forgive quickly, bitterness isn't allowed to make its nest in your heart. When you choose otherwise, the underpinnings for bitterness are established. Forgiveness invites God to pour out His blessings on your life. Unforgiveness invites Him to do the opposite.

Did you realize that when you are disobedient to God's Word, He will allow pressures to come into your life to press you back to Himself? This could be depression, frustration, bitterness, even illness brought on by stress. He may be pressing you to forgive right now as He did with a young woman we know, whose life, including her marriage, was affected by bitterness.

## The Less Loved Daughter

There is a second story about a less loved daughter, but this one has a different outcome. This woman's father had two daughters. For whatever reason, the father preferred the older daughter, and the younger child felt it. There came a day when she confronted her dad about this. He denied it, but it was true. Most everyone who knew the family noticed the favoritism, but the father refused to acknowledge it.

The father died with the issue unresolved, and in the following years the younger daughter grew increasingly depressed about her feelings toward her deceased dad.

One day she heard this specific teaching on forgiveness. As she walked to her car, she realized that she had never forgiven her father for showing favoritism to her sister. She could see that she was "imprisoned with torture."

As she was getting into her car and preparing to drive away, she decided it was time to face the facts. She drove straight to the cemetery and stood before her father's grave. There, alone, surrounded by her memories and her sorrow, she took action.

She asked God to forgive her unforgiveness toward her father. Then she directed her attention to his grave and said, "Dad, I forgive you." She later told a dear friend that at that moment the heavy burden she had been carrying was gone, laid to rest once and for all. She felt that it was a turning point in her life.

If someone has hurt you, and it has become an issue between you, it would be most appropriate to resolve the issue face-to-face. Many times, though, the other person is unaware of the way you feel. In such a case, prayerfully consider forgiving them without their knowledge.

We could give numerous examples of the freedom that forgiveness brings, but we are limited by the constraints of time and space. However, the one question we encourage you to ask yourself is, *"Are there people in my life, now or in the past, whom I've never forgiven?"* If there are, forgive them, and then ask God's forgiveness for your unforgiving heart.

*When you forgive quickly, bitterness isn't allowed to make its nest in your heart.*

Of course, there are many problems which are not caused by a woman's lack of forgiveness. A problem may exist in your marriage because of the willful disobedience of your spouse or others. God will deal with their disobedience. Your responsibility is to walk in obedience to Him regardless of another's actions.

## The Parable Concludes

At the conclusion of Jesus' parable, do you see that both men were imprisoned? The king never did release the servant who owed the meager debt, although we might have hoped He would. But what He did do was take action against a man who refused to give others what he himself had been given.

The parallel for us is that Christ died on the cross to forgive our sins. He forgave us a huge debt, our lifetime of sin, which is represented by the ten thousand talents in silver that the first servant owed the king. What He asks in return is for us to forgive others.

It was the predetermined plan and foreknowledge of God *that Jesus death on the cross would accomplish forgiveness for our sins* (Acts 2:23). Apart from His death, there would be no forgiveness, and therefore we would be separated eternally from God. But because of His death, we can look forward to spending eternity with Him if we've trusted Him as our Savior.

Prior to His crucifixion, Jesus was seized in the Garden of Gethsemane, bound, and arrested. He was beaten, flogged, and taunted. A crown of thorns was placed upon His head, and He was nailed to the cross. And there on Calvary's hill, before the Lamb of God died, all of our sins He was literally dying to forgive came upon Him. The minute, the instant, He gave up His spirit and died, forgiveness was achieved (John 1:29; 1 Corinthians 15:3; 2 Corinthians 5:21; Revelation 1:5).

Once you have put your trust in Christ, your salvation is never lost, but you can choose to live in the prison of unforgiveness. Galatians 5:1 says that you are set free for freedom! Why would you ever choose to give up your freedom through unforgiveness?

The price was so high; the payment so costly:

You were not redeemed with perishable things like silver or gold…, but with precious blood, as of a lamb unblemished and spotless, *the blood* of Christ. (1 Peter 1:18–19)

Don't hold your gift of freedom lightly. It cost Jesus everything!

## PRINCIPLE 4: FORGIVENESS IS YOUR BIRTHRIGHT

Are you extremely hard on yourself, especially in the area of forgiveness? Have you caused another a great deal of pain or sadness? Were you raised in a home where forgiveness was not extended easily, if at all? Perhaps, then, you have a difficult time receiving forgiveness from others and from God as well. You can forgive everyone else, but you can't forgive yourself.

If you are such a person, remember that *Jesus died on the cross for your sins.* They have been washed away…cleansed…covered. If you ask for His forgiveness, you receive it instantly. Accept it! *It has already been given to you by Him.* It is your birthright as a member of God's family. To not receive forgiveness, or to convince yourself that you aren't worthy of it, is to say that His death was not enough.

Through a friend, we know of a man who, in young adulthood, killed numerous people. He lived in the underworld and led a life far removed from what most of us could ever imagine. There came a time when he turned away from that life and began searching for something to hold onto. His despair only deepened, however, because he was haunted by his past. One day a stranger told him about the saving grace of Jesus Christ and how His death on the cross covered all his sins.

"But you don't understand my sins," the man cried out in pain. "How can God forgive me when I can't forgive myself?"

"You don't understand my Savior," the stranger replied. "Your sins, every single one of them, however heinous, have been washed clean by His blood." After further conversation, the man trusted

Jesus to be his Savior. The healing process had begun, and a sense of peace enveloped him.

Whatever it is you're hanging onto, it's time to let it go. Psalm 147:3 tells us that *He heals the brokenhearted and binds up their wounds.* Allow Jesus to heal your heartaches. Open the door to His peace.

All too often we project our own personality onto God. This is especially true of a person who forgives slowly. We think He is like us. *But He is not!* We don't have to perform prolonged acts of penance to receive His forgiveness, for no condemnation hangs over the heads of those who are His. The judge Himself has declared us free from sin. You are acceptable as a person because of what Jesus did on the cross. You are totally forgiven, no matter how great or recent a failure you've had to confess or how often you've failed.

You don't have to do anything to earn God's forgiveness, except confess your sin to Him. There is no reason to sink down into regret, shame, or denial or make excuses for what you've done. Simply tell Him and thank Him for His grace.

It is a wise woman who keeps short accounts with the Lord through a daily time of confession. He is faithful to His word, and He promises instant forgiveness. First John 1:9 tells us that "if we confess our sins, He is faithful and righteous to forgive us our sins and to cleanse us from all unrighteousness."

Jesus demonstrated this very thing when He washed his disciples' feet. He said that "he who has bathed needs only to wash his feet; but is completely clean" (John 13:10, NASB). If a person takes a bath, then walks barefoot into the yard to get the evening newspaper, he needs only to wash the grass and dust from his feet before going to bed. Spiritually, when you ask Jesus to be your Savior, you have been cleansed from sin, as in taking a bath. However, you will continue sinning from time to time. To be completely clean again, all you need to do is confess these sins before Jesus.

Not having a daily confession time results in feeling unclean and perhaps guilty. Never forget that guilt is a friend that takes you to the cross; once you have confessed your sins, its work is finished. If you continue to feel guilty over a sin that has been confessed, that feeling is *not* from God. There is nothing in your past that Jesus' death didn't cover. *Nothing.*

## PRINCIPLE 5: FORGIVENESS IS A CHOICE

It is a simple yet powerful thing to realize that forgiveness is a choice. You can choose to forgive out of obedience to Christ regardless of your feelings. If forgiveness were dependent on our feelings, we might well never forgive. Jesus' feelings had nothing to do with His obedience to His Father. Remember, He prayed, "My Father, if it is possible, let this cup pass from Me; yet not as I will, but as You will" (Matthew 26:39, NASB). Ultimately, one's life is based on the choices one makes. Forgiving others is *always* the right choice.

When you purchase a car, you must decide on the options you want. Do you want leather seats, sporty hubcaps, or four-wheel drive? In some cars, even the floor mats are optional.

Forgiveness isn't an option in a godly marriage, it is a *must*. It was meant to be standard equipment for the godly wife. Forgiveness puts the pieces back in place when they've been broken apart or blown to bits; it is the very cement that glues the heart together. Learning to forgive your mate for his shortcomings and oversights is critical if you want to become the wife that God intended you to become.

When we (Connie) were first married, if my husband said

anything that was critical or abrupt, I forgave him instantly. Many times I forgave him whether he asked my forgiveness or not, so eager was I to keep the channels of love and communication open. As the years went by, however, my eagerness dimmed, and that kind of instant forgiveness ceased to exist. I found myself feeling annoyed at little things, such as the way he squeezed the toothpaste or hung his towel. I had gone from a wife who forgave quickly to a wife who rarely forgave.

In short, I had become a full-time bookkeeper. I kept a record of everything my husband did that annoyed me. Or irritated me. Or frustrated me. I kept detailed accounts of all the things I did for him and all the things I thought he should be doing for me, but wasn't. I kept mental notes each time my feelings were hurt. I was extremely busy, and my accounting business was thriving, but my marriage was not.

As I grew in spiritual maturity, I would attempt to reconcile the records. I would forgive my husband, wipe the slate clean, and commit to starting over again. This would last anywhere from a few days to a few weeks, when, for whatever reason, I would feel offended once again. At that point I would reopen my accounting business and be busier than ever updating the files. How I had changed from the early days of my marriage, when my husband's happiness had meant the world to me.

I, like thousands of other women, always wondered why my marriage ran so hot and cold. For me, the issue at the root of this cycle was true, not temporary, forgiveness. Temporary forgiveness does not exist. To forgive temporarily is not really to forgive.

I had a wonderful grandmother who used to say, "No matter what happens to me in life, I hope I will always remember who I am." She thought that she could handle almost anything except losing her mental capabilities.

When I would hear her say this, I would think, "No matter what happens to me in life, I hope never to turn into a bitter woman." As a young girl, I found it fascinating to watch women and study what made them tick. I noticed that frequently as a woman aged, she seemed to become bitter and joyless. It was rare to find an older woman whose heart was joyful.

I was surprised and saddened to realize, at the ripe old age of thirty-five, that I had become the woman I had hoped never to resemble. It was only when I understood this principle of forgiveness *and chose to forgive* that I was able, by God's grace, to move forward in this area.

## PRINCIPLE 6: FORGIVENESS LEAVES THE CONSEQUENCES TO GOD

Choosing to forgive an offense doesn't mean that there aren't consequences for the offender, just that they don't come from *our* hand. The Bible instructs us to leave the consequences for the offender up to God.

> Never take your own revenge, beloved, but leave room for the wrath of God, for it is written, "Vengeance is Mine, I will repay," says the Lord. (Romans 12:19, NASB)

The consequences are to be decided by God, not us. Our refusing to take them into our own hands will clear the way for Him to deal with the offender.

Do not gloat when your enemy falls; when he stumbles, do not let your heart rejoice, or the Lord will see and disapprove and turn his wrath away from him. (Proverbs 24:17, NIV)

## PRINCIPLE 7: FORGIVENESS COLORS EVERYTHING

When I (Connie) was a young girl, I used to help my mother make angel food cakes from scratch. It seemed we beat those egg whites forever before they were just right. Once the batter was made, Mom would pour some of it into another bowl. Then she'd take a drop of red food coloring and make that batter pink. My sisters and I loved seeing the cake come out of the oven with a pink ring in the center.

It never ceased to amaze me how one tiny drop of coloring could color an entire bowl of batter. Similarly, when you choose to forgive, every area of your life is affected. Your thought life changes, and you no longer find yourself obsessing over who did what to whom. Not only does it alter the way you interact with the person involved, it most likely changes how you interact with others as well.

Forgiveness fosters growth in your Christian life and fine tunes your prayer life. It can literally change your appearance, improve your sleeping habits, and give you a renewed zest for life. Some people believe it is instrumental in relieving certain types of depression. It may also bring about reconciliation and resurrect dead or dying relationships. Forgiveness removes the heavy padlock of unforgiveness from your heart, and your life will bear witness to this in many ways.

Not long ago a friend told us that two members of her family hadn't spoken in almost twenty years due to differences of opinion regarding some farmland. Their farms adjoined each other's, and frequently their paths crossed, yet nary a word had passed between them since the dispute. The entire community was aware of the unfortunate situation.

One afternoon, one of the women picked up the phone and called the other.

"May I come over for a while tonight? I'd like to speak with you," she said.

"Yes, certainly you may," the other replied.

The two women met that night. After a few awkward moments, the first said, "I'm not even sure what happened way back then, but whatever it was, I'd like to ask your forgiveness." The other woman concurred. Since that day, the two have shared a close relationship. As one woman said to a friend, "Forgiveness touched everything in my life. Even my food tastes better!"

Did you notice how the first woman took the initiative in seeking forgiveness? *This is key, and it is the most mature thing we can do as Christian women.* We must take the initiative in resolving conflicts.

Forgiveness colors and enriches every aspect of your life. *And so does unforgiveness.* When you choose to forgive, you'll discover how God blesses a forgiving spirit. But He *cannot and will not* bless an unforgiving one. Won't you, today, allow the beautiful hue of forgiveness to color your life?

## CLARIFICATIONS

In talking with women, and from our own personal experiences, we have discovered that often forgiveness is seen through a distorted

*Take the initiative in seeking forgiveness.*

lens, which causes confusion and uncertainty. Below is a clarification of what forgiveness does not necessarily entail:

1. Forgiveness doesn't always mean reconciliation. In order for reconciliation to occur, trust must be reestablished. This requires cooperation and true repentance from the offender. Since the actions of another are essential for reconciliation, there is no guarantee that this will happen.

2. Forgiveness isn't necessarily forgetting. How often have we heard the phrase "Forgive and forget"? To forgive others as God forgave us implies forgetting. We feel this should be our goal. However, in our human state, we will often remember the event and the resulting pain. We can, though, refuse to let these memories cripple, embitter, or weaken our faith. One might be surprised to find that the memory of the offense fades as time goes by.

3. Forgiveness isn't excusing or tolerating. You aren't required to make excuses for another's poor behavior (they didn't know better, they didn't have the advantages I had, they practically raised themselves, etc.). Everyone is responsible before God for his or her actions and may well suffer consequences as a result of them.

4. Forgiveness isn't dependent upon another's acceptance of it. There may be times when you forgive another, but he or she refuses to accept your forgiveness. This doesn't negate the sincerity of your forgiveness in any way.

5. Forgiveness isn't making certain others forgive you. You can

seek forgiveness from others, but whether they choose to give it or not is up to them. *You aren't responsible for another's forgiveness.* Don't allow this to emotionally imprison you.

## CHRIST'S FINAL WORDS TO ANOTHER

Before dying on the cross, Christ's final words to another human being were words of forgiveness. Luke tells us of this last precious conversation between a mortal man—a thief, no less—and the immortal Christ.

> One of the criminals who hung there hurled insults at him: "Aren't you the Christ? Save yourself and us!"
>
> But the other criminal rebuked him. "Don't you fear God," he said, "since you are under the same sentence? We are punished justly, for we are getting what our deeds deserve. But this man has done nothing wrong."
>
> Then he said, "Jesus, remember me when you come into your kingdom."
>
> Jesus answered him, "I tell you the truth, today you will be with me in paradise." (Luke 23:39–43, NIV)

The thief saw with his own eyes, from his unique vantage point that Jesus was dying on the cross, bleeding from all He had endured. Yet the thief realized that this was the Son of God and belived that He would come into His kingdom. Amazingly, the thief came to a decision in the very last moments of his life, asking Christ to remember him in His resurrection.

After all He had endured—the betrayals, the beatings, the

floggings, the spitting, the insults, the utter horror of it all—Jesus heard the thief and responded, literally, with open arms.

With gentleness and compassion, He said to him, "I tell you the truth, today you will be with me in paradise." The thief, in his final few moments of life, was forgiven.

We often want to forgive, but only if it comes easily, especially in our marriages. If it is a difficult situation, or the circumstances are especially hurtful, we want to step back, nurse our wounds, and think it over. Christ didn't do that. He didn't step back. Instead, He allowed His feet to be nailed to a cross. He didn't nurse His wounds, and they were far deeper and more painful than yours or ours. He thought over only one thing: whether or not He was doing the will of His Father.

How long has it been since you've considered doing God's will regarding forgiving another? His desire is for you to forgive. Over and over and over again. Are you a forgiving person? Would you consider following God's plan for your life in this area?

The hallmark of Jesus' life was forgiveness.

It was the reason He was born.

It was the reason He lived.

It was the reason that He died.

Is forgiveness a hallmark of your life? Through Christ, you can forgive others, and you can humbly ask others to forgive you. And you can know that by doing so, you are becoming more and more like Jesus!

## CHAPTER 3 SUMMARY

1.  Accept Christ's forgiveness and forgive others in the same way.

2.  What we don't forgive may come back into our own lives at some point.

3.  There is no such thing as partial forgiveness. Failing to forgive fully is not forgiving at all.

4.  When you've offended someone, ask their forgiveness.

5.  When someone has offended you, grant them forgiveness, *whether they ask your forgiveness or not.*

6.  Don't ask yourself whether the other person deserves your forgiveness. We didn't deserve Christ's forgiveness, yet He forgave us; by the same principle we are commanded to forgive others.

7. Forgiveness doesn't mean that you weren't hurt; it means that you are choosing to leave the consequences to God.

8. Forgiveness doesn't necessarily mean that reconciliation will occur, that you will forget what happened, or that you should excuse or tolerate the sins of others.

9. Forgiveness doesn't depend on whether another person receives it; nor does it mean that you must convince another to offer it to you.

10. Forgiveness was the hallmark of Christ's life. Is it a hallmark of yours?

A few years ago, my (Connie) aunt suffered a massive stroke. Because I lived just a few hours away, I decided to drive to the hospital to be with the family for a day.

The city was large and unfamiliar to me. I became lost and found myself in a remote, deserted area. My three-year-old daughter was with me, and I was nervous and afraid.

Finally, after several blocks, I drove out of that section of town, and there in front of me stood the hospital for which I was searching. My muscles relaxed, and relief flooded my body.

I visited with my cousins, and that evening when it came time to leave, I dreaded the prospect of finding my way back to the interstate. "Stay close to us," my cousins said. "We'll lead you to the interstate."

I stayed so close to them they thought our bumpers were connected. There was no way I was going to let them out of my sight. Because of their leading, my return trip was easy.

Staying close to my cousins altered my trip home. What do you suppose would happen if we stayed close to our King?

This is called abiding, and there's nothing else like it on earth! You'll find your relationship with Jesus to be more intimate when you do this and discover a peace and contentment that you didn't have before. And it will make your trip "home" far richer, as well!

*Abiding in Christ—are you close to your King?*

# CHAPTER FOUR

# Abiding
# in Christ

*Abiding is the heartbeat
of the Christian walk.*

**H**ome. The very word should bring to your mind a sense of security and peace. It is a place that you can retreat to and be revived. The ideal home is where you experience another's unconditional love and have someone's undivided attention. The welcome mat is always at the door, and even as you approach you can almost see arms opened wide to embrace you.

When either of us have family and friends visit, we make an extra effort to show them our love. The guest room is made ready with handmade quilts on the bed and extra ones nearby in case they need additional warmth. We might set out a tray that holds a teapot and teacups and perhaps a vase with fresh flowers. Along with this, we make sure there is plenty of reading material available—a daily devotional, books of interest, perhaps a new magazine or two.

I (Nancy) have a tall tree decorated with little white lights that stands in the corner of my guest room. At night I draw a bath for my loved one. I have a tray that stretches across the tub, and on it I place lighted candles and a cup of tea. A pillow to rest the head upon is at the back of the tub, and nearby is a small tape recorder which plays soft music. We often give our guests inexpensive items that will serve as a reminder of our time together. This attention to their comfort touches them, and it delights us when we are privileged to welcome guests into our home.

We can, for a day or two, bring refreshment to another—but being *at home in Christ* is to be cared for twenty-four hours a day, year round.

You cannot be a helper to your husband the way God intended apart from abiding in Christ. Abiding impacts everything in your life—not only your marriage, but everything! When you focus on Christ instead of your husband, something inexplicable and marvelous happens to you. Your role as helper becomes not only possible, it becomes thrilling as well!

When you come to Him, Jesus says you will find
rest...
    relief...
        ease...
            refreshment...
                recreation
                    and blessed quiet for your souls.
                        (Matthew 11:28–30, AMP)

I (Nancy) have visited some of the great homes of the world. I've stood in front of the White House in Washington, D.C., but the ones who lived there didn't welcome me in as their guest. When I walked by the Palace of the Emperor in Tokyo, Japan, I wasn't even noticed. As I visited Buckingham Palace in London, to my amazement Queen Elizabeth and her husband rode by in a horse-drawn carriage. She even waved to me. But she did not stop to invite me in. There is a royal home, however, where the door is not only open, but where you are invited to be forever.

## A ROYAL HOME

Did you know you can have a permanent place in a royal home? You can. It is Jesus Himself who initiates this most intimate relationship you can have with Him. It is the home that Jesus freely gives to those who have responded to His initial call, "Come and follow Me." He says:

> "Abide in Me, live in Me, make your home in Me, just as I do in you." (John 15:4, NASB, paraphrased)

When you come home to Him, you will find what you have been looking for all your life. When you are at home in Christ, you experience His wholehearted love and complete attention. He notices your weariness. He sees when you are heavy laden and overburdened. When the worries of the world seem to overwhelm you, He is always ready to comfort and strengthen you.

A. W. Tozer speaks of this abiding faith walk as "the gaze of the soul on God."[1] Perhaps you have seen a field of sunflowers at a point in the day where their faces are pointed upwards, basking in the warmth of the sun. They are not pointed downwards or sideways, but stand fully upright, open wide to the heavens. When our hearts are like this, basking in His radiance and glory, longing to do what pleases Him, we are *abiding*.

*When you are at home in Christ, you will find what you've been looking for all your life.*

To abide means to stay in the same place with the same person. It is a life of sweet companionship with Christ. Abiding is an interactive partnership between almighty God and a believer. An abider depends on God and focuses on His strength, His sufficiency, and His enabling power.

In the book, *Daily With the King,* abiding is described as three things:

A conscious awareness of His presence at all times. That does not mean direct verbal communication with Him, but the feeling that He is there, as a child playing is aware of its mother's nearby presence.

Second, it also means a careful consultation with Him about everything that affects us. That consultation may be in direct prayer, or else in scanning the Bible indirectly for any message He has for us there. The important thing is to keep the lines of communication open with Him so that we are instantly ready to receive any necessary message sent from Him.

Third, it means a continual enjoyment of Him as a

person. That means He is a joy, a delight to us at all times; the very thought of Him fills us with pleasure."[2]

This abiding relationship is open to all believers, but many are uncertain how they can have it. Sadly, many who do understand this principle are unwilling to give what Jesus requires.

## THE COST

If you keep My commandments, you will abide in My love, just as I have kept my Father's commandments, and abide in His love. (1 John 15:10, NASB)

The requirement for abiding is obedience to the Father. That is how you remain in fellowship with Christ. That is also the way to walk as He walked, which is what we are challenged to do: "The one who says he abides in Him ought himself to walk in the same manner as He walked" (1 John 2:6, NASB).

Obedience is submission to the authority of God. As you read your Bible, do you apply what you are learning to your own life? When you see areas in your life that need to be changed, do you commit to changing them, or do you instead try to figure out reasons why it's okay to continue living as you are?

Do you recall wanting your own way when you were a small child and how your parents tried to keep you from the dangers that might have developed if you had gotten it? "Don't run into the street!" "Don't talk to strangers!" "Don't touch the oven, the plug, the spider...." Sometimes they told you why, and other times they just said, "Don't!"

I (Nancy) can remember my own father's instructions: "Nan, don't do such and so," he would tell me. Always, I would ask why. Sometimes he would tell me, and other times he'd simply say, "Because I have a reason."

There is always a perfect reason to be obedient to God. Sometimes the answer is obvious, other times one chooses to obey only because God said so, even though His reasons may be unclear.

*The requirement for abiding is obedience to the Father.*

I (Connie) was a Christian for many years before I began to understand the principle of abiding. Prior to that, I thought abiding was about a few verses in the Bible rather than an ongoing, intimate walk with Jesus. But one day I finally got it. It became crystal clear as when a lens suddenly becomes focused. It was then that I fully understood that the cost of abiding was obedience.

*And I was so disappointed!* I felt weary, and I had just begun. Obedience to me was a plodding kind of word. It reminded me of a workhorse toiling along in the field, with endless acres of soil to turn. Row after row the horse trudges, straining to pull the heavy plow. I am grieved to admit this, but that is how I felt.

Only later, as I began to practice obedience, did I discover how sorely mistaken I had been. Obedience isn't a plodding kind of thing. It isn't trudging along, as I had thought. *Obedience is what frees you to run!* It is the very thing that brings you into a warm, close relationship with Jesus. Once you discover the sweet taste of obedience, you will no longer want to settle for less.

So often we want to experience the blessings of obedience without obeying. We want fulfilled marriages without being excellent wives. We want personal satisfaction and joy, but we want the option of dragging our heels whenever we feel like it. We want to know God's will for our lives, but we're too busy to sit at His feet to discover just what that is. Many want to be godly, but few are willing to be obedient. Yet this is the very thing on which abiding hinges. Obedience opens the door to an understanding of who God is and shows us more and more fully what His will for our lives is.

God instructed Noah to build an ark of enormous proportions in an era that had yet to see rain. This was no small project. It took over one hundred years and was done at a time when the wickedness of man was great. But Noah abided in the presence of God—in fact, the Bible says he walked with God. His wasn't a crisis faith. His faith was deep long *before* the flood. Noah's was a major and lengthy task, but he carried it out because God had told Him to, even though it may have seemed an odd command at the time. In essence, it was Noah's personal obedience to God's word that saved not only himself, *but his family as well.* After the rains, they became the only humans on earth. Your presence on this earth bears witness to Noah's obedience.

Abiding is where you experience the reality of God's fathomless love. Andrew Murray states, "Abiding in Jesus is nothing but the giving up of oneself to be ruled and taught and led, and so resting in the arms of Everlasting Love."[3]

We have a friend who lived a seemingly successful, fulfilling life. In his late forties he was a successful businessman who was widely respected. Recently, however, he felt a restlessness in his spirit and sensed a void in his life. One day he approached a man in his office, whom he knew to be a Christian, though he wasn't sure what that meant. "There's got to be more to life than what I'm experiencing," he told the man. "I have everything I ever thought I could want, yet something is missing. Can you teach me about the Bible?"

Of course, the man in his office was more than happy to do this! He told our friend about Jesus, and our friend made the decision to ask Him to be his personal Savior, which is the first step to abiding. In that instant, his life was changed! He began to pray and ask God to reveal Himself to him. Yearning to know more about his Savior, he became active in a Bible study. He began spending time with God and found a peace that he had never before known. Now, not only does he reside in a lovely earthly residence, he abides in a place far more beautiful: a royal home that gives him what his earthly home cannot. He is now *at home* in Christ.

## THE PLUMB LINE

If you've ever hung wallpaper, you know that one of the first things you do is put up a plumb line. This is a piece of string with a weight at one end. You nail this weighted cord to the seam where the ceiling meets the wall. Then you put the first sheet of wallpaper exactly where the cord is hanging. By doing this, the wallpaper will be straight.

The plumb line for your life is the Word of God. It is when your behavior is lined up with what He reveals in the Bible that you become straight with God. This is called obedience, and it is the front door to abiding. There is no other entrance.

Years ago, as a new Christian, all of this talk about obedience surprised me (Nancy). I remember thinking I'd have to give up many of the things I enjoyed. One was a "hobby" I had stumbled into called anger.

This hobby was thriving when I learned that the sun shouldn't go down on my anger (Ephesians 4:26). My walk with Christ was so new that my first thought was, "What fun is that?" I wasn't sure I could do it since anger had become such a big part of me. If someone hurt my feelings, I would become withdrawn and quiet until they seemed sorry enough for the offense. Because of my desire to abide in Christ, I set a goal: to get over my anger by sundown. I would actually peer out the window to see how much time I had left before having to give up my anger. Just as the sun was disappearing for the day, I would force myself to forgive the person. As the weeks went by, this seemed more trouble than it was worth. I soon began forgiving more and more quickly—even in the daylight! I couldn't believe the freedom that my obedience brought me. I experienced Christ's love for me in a deeper way and felt it increasingly as I began obeying in other areas of my life.

## THE OUTCOME

Jesus says when you abide in Him and in His love, the outcome will be joy. His actual words are:

> "My joy may be in you and that your joy may be made full." (John 15:11, NASB)

Are you joyful? If not, do you now know why? *His joy is extended to abiders.* Abiders are obeyers; obeyers are choosers. They choose to do what God says. They place their faith in Him as Noah did, regardless of whether they fully understand the command or feel like doing it at the moment.

What are the results of faith in God—coming to the Father through Jesus?

It stirs your love for Him and His Word.

Obedience grows out of love for Jesus and His word.

This opens the door to abiding,

which is the foundation for experiencing

*His* peace…

*His* love…

*His* joy!

(John 14:21, 27; 15:9, 11)

## Fruitfulness

Jesus goes on to say that as you abide in Him, you will bear fruit:

> "As the branch cannot bear fruit by itself unless it abides in the vine, so neither can you unless you abide in Me; I am the vine, you are the branches; he who abides in Me and I in him, he bears much fruit, for apart from Me you can do nothing." (John 15:4–5, NASB)

Fruit is the outcome of your obedience to Christ, and it is dependent on your choice to abide. The fruit of the Spirit is love, joy, peace, patience, kindness, goodness, faithfulness, gentleness, and self-control (Galatians 5:22–23). As you learn to abide more and more in Christ, the greater the fruitbearing will be in your life.

He is the vine; you are the branch. You cannot bear fruit apart from Him, just as a branch cannot bear fruit apart from the vine.

Stop reading for a moment and think about this. It is one of the most profound truths in Scripture, and it affects all that you are and all that you do. *Apart from Christ you have no power to live a victorious life.*

The friend we mentioned earlier bore lots of earthly fruit from his labors, but he bore no spiritual fruit before he asked Jesus to be his Savior. He couldn't, for he was living apart from Christ.

Are you availing yourself of the power Jesus so freely offers? Do you know how to activate that power? *It is a simple thing to do.* If a fan isn't plugged in, it is unable to circulate air, for it has no power apart from the electricity which runs it. It is able to work only after it's plugged into an electrical source.

Similarly, if you aren't abiding in Christ, you have salvation through Him, but you have no power to be fruitful and joyful. With Him living in you, and you in Him, you have all the power and resources you need to do this, not only in your marriage, but in the rest of your life as well. Christ is in you constantly through the presence of the Holy Spirit. This is what is meant by the Spirit-filled life.

Abiding in Christ is the only way to be a Christlike woman and wife. We cannot overemphasize the simplicity and reality of this promise. If you don't grasp this partnership, you will become discouraged because you will have no strength to live a victorious life.

Warren and Ruth Myers said, "We find a night and day difference in our lives when we choose against struggling to be strong and peaceful and loving—and instead, count on the strength and peace and love of Christ's life within us."[4]

Hudson Taylor, a famous missionary to China, struggled to abide. One day he received a letter from John McCarthy. One particular sentence from McCarthy's letter removed the scales from his eyes: "But how to get faith strengthened? Not by striving after faith, but by resting on the Faithful One." "Ah, there is rest!" thought Taylor, "I have striven in vain to rest in Him. I'll strive no more. For has He not promised to abide with me—never to leave me, never to fail me?"[5]

So often, we try to perform the work of the Spirit ourselves. We live in an age that says if we just work hard enough, we can accomplish anything. But we will never accomplish something that God Himself was meant to do. *He* is the vine; we are the branches. As we cling to *Him, He* produces the fruit in us.

My (Connie) family always had a vegetable garden, and my sisters and I spent time tending it. One of our jobs was to pick the ripened red tomatoes. Sometimes, though, we'd accidentally hit against a green tomato that wasn't ready to be picked. If we hit it hard enough to jar it loose from the vine, it no longer received nourishment and withered and died.

That's the idea here. When we allow ourselves to become detached or loosened from His Word through disobedience, fruit is no longer produced in our lives. Our salvation is still assured, but there is no fruit.

## YOUR PART

What is your part in abiding? You need to depend on and surrender to Jesus Christ:

*Dependence:* looking to Him, trusting Him for present power, resting in His love. *Surrender:* acknowledging that you can do *nothing* apart from Him and that you need His help and power.

Too often we think that trying harder is the answer to our problems—that this will dissolve the roadblocks and barriers in our marriage and in life in general. I (Connie) did this for years. On my good days, I was willing to try harder; on my bad days, I expected my husband to. But trying harder isn't the answer because *you* aren't the source of power that is needed for a changed life. *Christ* is, and it is He working in you through the Holy Spirit who will do this.

Returning to the example of the fan, your trying harder would be like plugging the fan into an electrical outlet that is dead. From all outward appearances, the fan ought to work, but it never will because there is no power available to cause the fan to whirl to life. You can turn the switch to the on position as often as you like, but the fan will remain motionless until it's plugged into a true source of power.

Similarly, you can continue trying harder for as long as you like, but nothing will happen, because there is no real power from which to draw. You're relying on yourself for power that only Christ can give. Fruit will only be produced in your life as you draw from Christ's strength, not your own. You simply cooperate through obedience.

How can you get in the habit of being aware that Christ is in you and with you? How can you begin cooperating through obedience? An excellent way to begin is with prayer, because abiding is the prerequisite for effective prayer.

## PRAYER

"If you abide in Me, and My words abide in you, ask whatever you wish, and it will be done for you" (John 15:7, NASB). Abiding encourages us to ask Jesus for anything. In their book, *31 Days of Prayer,* Ruth and Warren Myers say:

> As your hand experiences the life of your body as its own, so as you abide in Christ you experience the life of Christ as your own. Life that is fresh, pure, joyous, fruitful, free of anxiety, and full of faith. Life that is wrapped up in the desires that are in God's heart. Then when you pray, you express His longings; you want what He wants. And so He does what you ask." [6]

As you abide in Christ, His desires take precedence over yours. The more you abide, the more you will see this fully and begin to desire the things of God. What you want becomes secondary to what God wants for you. As you abide in Him, your wants begin to mirror His.

So often we invite God to become a part of *our* plan. And we feel generous and spiritual for doing so. This is completely backwards. There have been many times in our lives when we have prayed, "Lord, You know I'm going to start doing such and so tomorrow. I ask You to be a part of it." What we needed to do was ask God whether He even wanted us involved in the project. As you begin abiding, you'll stop making plans of your own and hoping or expecting Him to join you in them. Through prayer, you'll go directly to Him and seek His plans for your life.

Prayer is simply talking to God. You might begin to pray something like this:

*Lord, I often forget that You are with me, in me.*
*Help me today to develop this as a habit. Amen.*

As your day unfolds, send up frequent prayers to the Lord. These might be something such as:

*Lord, You are with me, You live within me.*
*The children will be home soon, please give me all*
*that I need to tenderly welcome them.*

*Lord, I am working. I have deadlines to meet. I feel*
*stress with a coworker. I ask for Your wisdom.*

*Lord, my husband seems removed and quiet. Please love*
*him through me. Help me reach out and comfort him.*

*Lord, I am in a situation where gossip abounds. Help me to*
*not contribute to this. Help me to guard the reputation of my*
*husband. Help me to turn this conversation to another path.*

As you send "arrow" prayers to the Lord throughout the day, your mind will be renewed, as will your heart and your strength. These prayers, however, cannot take the place of a concentrated prayer time with God. As you pray, you will gain a new perspective—an eternal perspective—and feel the presence of the Lord filling you as you commit your day and all that unfolds to Him.

## BEGINNING YOUR DAY

How do you begin your day? Do you stay in bed until the last second and then rush to get yourself and your family ready?

Try beginning it with prayer. Make a decision today to make a quiet time with the Lord a priority as you begin your day. There are some practical things we do to help us have "blanket victory" —victory over blankets and a cozy bed!

1. Ask the Lord to awaken you Himself. It is amazing how often you will suddenly find yourself wide awake at your requested time.

2. Make coffee the night before, using an automatic timer. When you begin your prayer time, the coffee is freshly made and ready for you. If you're not a coffee drinker, you might enjoy a steaming cup of hot tea, which takes just seconds to make.

3. If you need an alarm, put it out of reach, perhaps on your dresser or outside your door. This way you'll have taken the first five steps out of bed, which are the most difficult, and you'll have obtained forward momentum.

4. Consider getting up fifteen to twenty minutes before your family. This will ease you gently into your morning and allow you a few minutes of time with the Lord before beginning your day.

5. Begin prayer on your knees, if it is physically possible for you. We find this position reminds us of the holiness of God. It also quickens us as to our need for Him and helps us acknowledge that we are surrendered to Him.

6. Keep your Bible and devotionals in a basket or box next to your prayer spot. This will prevent a frantic search for them in the morning.

7. Faithfully read God's Word and be obedient to it. Jesus said:

"If anyone loves me, he will obey my teaching. My Father will love him, and we will come to him and make our home with him." (John 14:23, NIV)

8. Consider journaling. Write a few sentences in a notebook. Our journal entries vary. Sometimes we write purely to praise God or to thank Him. Other times it is about a problem that we are facing. Our writing style is simple and conversational. We both have a place in our journals where we keep written prayer requests for family, friends, those in Christian service, our own ministries, and worldwide needs. Highlight His answers to prayer with a colored marker. Soon you will see you own journal peppered with color!

If you are unaccustomed to a regular prayer time, you might be wondering how to begin. Many people divide their prayer time using the acrostic ACTS.

> A — Adore God; acknowledge who He is
> (Hebrews 13:15).
> C — Confess your sins (1 John 1:9).
> T — Thank Him for what He has done in your life
> (1 Thessalonians 5:18).
> S — Supplication: Pray for yourself and others
> (James: 5:16).

You may want to read a passage of Scripture. Devotionals are also helpful in giving direction for this time. We've listed three devotionals we recommend.

1. *Daily Light for Every Day* by Anne Graham Lotz, (J. Countryman).
2. *31 Days of Praise* by Ruth Myers, (Multnomah Publishers, Inc.).
3. *31 Days of Prayer* by Ruth and Warren Myers, (Multnomah Publishers, Inc.).

There are a number of devotionals other than these that you might enjoy. Ask your pastor and friends what they use. Visit your local Christian bookstore. Regardless of what you find, though, don't let anything take the place of your prayer time with God or reading from His Word.

## PRACTICE

It takes approximately three weeks to form a habit. If you want to be increasingly aware that Jesus is in you and that you are in Him, put reminders of this around your home and office. Set a timer to go off every hour for a few days, and when it does, thank Him for His presence and for what He's doing in your life. Put a post-it on your makeup mirror or your refrigerator door. Put your watch on backwards, with the time facing away from you. Your heart will overflow with love as you increasingly train your mind to be on Him.

Abiding in Christ is a powerful thing. As you abide, you will find yourself responding to your husband and others differently. Frequently their responses will also change as they witness the Holy Spirit at work in your life.

Sadly, one can slip out of abiding with Christ. Several things can cause this: disobedience, pride, and unforgiveness, to mention a few. Another common cause is allowing hurt feelings to rule behavior.

## PAINTING AND ABIDING

It was late October, and my (Connie) husband and I were trying to finish painting our home before winter set in. As the afternoon wound down, dark clouds appeared overhead. A rainstorm appeared imminent, but we decided that if we hurried, we could get the garage painted before the storm hit.

We painted as quickly as we could, racing against the clouds. Just as we finished the last board, large raindrops began to fall. The paint was water based and hadn't dried. As the rain hit the fresh paint, it began to run. Within minutes, the entire area was streaked and looked far worse than it did originally. Not only that, but the old paint had begun to peel anew and would have to be prepped again—a long, arduous task.

The rains were short-lived and the sun reappeared, quickly drying the wet wood. My husband worked for over an hour to get the area ready to be repainted. He then left for his evening shift at work.

He came home the next morning exhausted. After eating a quick bite of breakfast, he headed to our room to sleep. Early in the afternoon, a thought hit me. I would surprise him by repainting the ruined area. Even though there were once again ominous looking clouds overhead, I began.

*Surely it won't rain two afternoons in a row,* I said to myself. It was a foolish thought, for the clouds were darker than they'd been on the previous day.

Unbelievably, just as I was finishing the same board, I felt a raindrop hit. In dismay I looked up into the sky just as the rain came pouring down. I quickly gathered up my supplies and headed indoors. Though disappointed, I knew my husband would be touched by my efforts.

A bit later, my husband awoke and came into the kitchen. I showed him how I had attempted to repaint the wall. The day was dark and gloomy and the rain continued falling as we talked.

"Was it cloudy like this when you began?" he asked.

"Yes," I said, laughing, "but I thought that this time I could surely beat the rain."

"I wish you hadn't done that," he said in frustration. "Now I have to prep the wood for a third time. From now on, if there are rain clouds in the sky, *don't paint.*"

It seemed to me that my husband was doing far more scolding than he was commending. I was expecting him to be moved by my actions, and he was! But not in the way I had expected.

My feelings were hurt. I couldn't understand his response. Although I wasn't consciously thinking of this at the time, what I decided to do was to bear a grudge against him for the rest of the evening. I was cool and aloof. Later that night, he again left for his job. There was an uneasiness in my spirit as there always is when I cease abiding and allow hurt feelings to dictate my behavior. I tried to dismiss it and went to bed.

*Sadly, one can slip out of abiding in Christ. A common cause is allowing hurt feelings to rule behavior.*

Early the next morning, I got out of bed for my quiet time with the Lord. The restlessness was still there. I asked Jesus to reveal to me anything I needed to correct in regard to the paint issue. Instantly, I felt convicted that my grudge-bearing and cool attitude had been wrong and that my pride needed to be replaced with humility.

"Humility, Lord?" I asked. "Why are you pressing me to be humble when *he* is at fault?" I might as well have been in the Garden with Eve, for I was trying to blame someone else for my sin.

As I sat at His feet and talked with Him, I realized that as long as I called myself His, I was called to be humble. It is the very essence of who He is, and it should be the same for me. How easy it is to push this aside when pride and hurt feelings kick in.

As I prayed, the Lord gave me a glimpse into my own heart. What a mess it was. It is easy to let yourself off the hook if you are constantly looking for the wrong in others. I was grieved at my behavior. I asked the Lord's forgiveness and knew I needed to do the same of my husband. About that time the back door opened. My husband, remembering my mood from the previous evening, briefly acknowledged me and headed to our room to sleep.

"Wait!" I said, "I need to say something." He came back to where I was and sat down in the chair beside me.

"I'm so sorry I was cold toward you last night. I was wrong. Will you forgive me?"

His spirit softened instantly. "I was wrong, too," he said, "but when I looked out at the wet paint, all I could see was the time it would take to prep it again. Plus I was tired from working nights. I'm sorry."

His entire body seemed to relax then. He leaned back in the chair and began talking about his previous night at work. He works in a busy hospital and during his shift, a couple had come in holding their nonresponsive baby in their arms. Though the medical staff did all it could, the baby couldn't be revived. My husband talked about how sad the parents were, and his eyes misted as he spoke of our own children sleeping peacefully just a few rooms away. He shared how inadequate he felt trying to comfort the grieving parents.

He went on to speak of a second case in which a young man had tried to commit suicide. The man said he felt helpless, hopeless, and had no reason to live. My husband sat and talked with him and told him about Someone who gave hope. The man repented of his sins and trusted Jesus to be his Savior. My husband's eyes lit up, and a smile crossed his face as he told me this news. He then went to get some rest.

Had I not sought the Lord, I feel sure I wouldn't have apologized so quickly, if at all. I would have continued holding on to my hurt. My husband would have gone straight to bed, and a wonderful opportunity of sharing would have been lost.

This is just one example of what can happen as you abide in Christ. He equips you to bear fruit. Apart from Him, you can do *nothing*.

Familiarize yourself with the red flags that indicate you are no longer abiding. These might include a critical spirit, thoughts of revenge, indifference, cold treatment toward another, unforgiveness, grudge-bearing, and primarily, no longer spending time with God—or doing so in a rushed, "have-to" manner.

In a letter to believers in Galatia, Paul said, "You were running a good race. Who cut in on you and kept you from obeying the truth? That kind of persuasion *does not* come from the one who calls you" (Galatians 5:7–8, NIV). Purpose to abide in the One who called you. Should you discover that you are no longer abiding, run to Him! Ask Him to help you begin abiding again.

## ABIDING IS FOUNDATIONAL

Women often want their marriages to change, but they have no idea that this has anything to do with abiding. It has everything to do with it! *Abiding is foundational to what you want.*

Many think of marriage as one compartment of their lives and abiding as another. They separate the two. They feel compelled to work on the barriers in their marriage, yet never consider this principle of abiding. What they don't realize is that the two *cannot* be separated.

*Everything in your life is affected when you abide!* When you are truly at home in Christ, it will transcend all that you do. Regardless of the trials you are facing currently, the first step to facing them is to abide in Christ, drawing on His strength and wisdom.

Will your marriage be improved if you abide? This can't be predicted because it involves the choices of another person. However, *every* aspect of *your* life will be colored by your choosing to do so. We encourage you to abide continually in Christ, not only as you endeavor to strengthen your marriage, but in your everyday life as well.

## NOT SOMEHOW, BUT TRIUMPHANTLY

Every few years when the Olympics come around, we enjoy watching women's gymnastics. The balance beam is considered by most to be the toughest of the four apparatuses. The competitors perform all sorts of jumps, turns, and whirls on the narrow board, but the overriding goal is to *stay on the beam*. Many will get off balance just a tiny bit, and you can see them fighting to stay atop the beam, using every muscle available to keep from falling.

Abiding is similar to this. You want to abide—stay atop the beam—*regardless!* You may stumble and trip, and life may throw some real challenges your way, but no matter what, *stay on the beam!* Don't allow anything—pride, anger, rejection, hurt, unforgiveness—to cause you to fall. If you do, get up quickly and *get back on the beam!*

A. Wetherell Johnson, a woman whose love for the Lord impacts thousands of lives, believed that through abiding in Christ, you can live "not somehow, but triumphantly."[7]

Don't those words have a beautiful ring? You can do it through abiding. The "somehow" of your life will slowly give way to "triumphant" as you hand the worn and tattered oars over to the One who powers the boat.

Aren't you tired of rowing? There's no reason to any longer. A stronger set of arms is waiting to hold you, enfold you, and direct the course of your life from this point forward.

"Not somehow, but triumphantly!" May this be your heart's desire as you seek to abide in Him.

"Not somehow, but triumphantly!" May you settle for nothing less.

## CHAPTER 4 SUMMARY

1. Being *at home in Christ* is to be cared for twenty-four hours a day.

2. When you come home to Him, you will find what you've been looking for all your life.

3. Abiding is an interactive partnership between almighty God and a believer.

4. The cost of abiding is obedience to His Word.

5. Obedience is submission to the authority of God.

6. The plumb line for your life is the Word of God.

7. Obedience is the front door to abiding—there is no other entrance.

8. Obedience brings freedom, and once you discover its sweet taste, you won't want to settle for less anymore.

9. The outcome of abiding is fruitfulness and joy.

10. Effective prayer requires abiding, for it is only as you abide that your wants begin to mirror His.

# Part 3

# The Job
# Description

Submission in marriage. If you want to heat up a conversation, simply mention those words. We attended a large gathering recently, and this topic was mentioned. Various things were being discussed all around us, but once these words were spoken, they spread like wildfire through the room. Within seconds, most everyone was debating someone else on the topic. People jockeyed to get the floor, and no sooner would someone begin to speak, than someone else would interrupt or correct. Until this time, the mood of the party had been pleasant and understated, but now emotion ran rampant. "I'd say someone hit a nerve," a friend mused wryly, "a raw nerve."

A raw nerve indeed. In writing this book, we spoke with dozens of women on a number of subjects. Yet none generated the controversy that submission did. Many chaffed at the mere mention of the word. Said one woman, "I can barely stand to hear 'that' word spoken aloud." We found this to be a common reaction among Christian and non-Christian women alike. Wary and cautious, today's woman is uncertain whether submission any longer fits into her lifestyle. In this chapter, we hope to clearly delineate what God says about this issue and exhort you to consider if your stand lines up with God's plan!

*Submission in marriage—God's design for your best.*

# CHAPTER FIVE

# Order in the Home

*Submission: great strength*
*harnessed for the glory of God!*

He was the last one off of the plane. When his wife, holding their younger daughter, saw him, she ran to his open arms. They were oblivious to the people waiting to board. Their embrace was deeply touching and prolonged.

Lingering behind was their older daughter, about six years of age. As soon as Dad could let go of Mom, he knelt and swept her into a bear hug. They were lost in their own world.

Then Dad began to reach for the small daughter still in her mother's arms—but she wouldn't go to him. Mom kept turning this way and that so he could see her, but she was covering her eyes with her hands. She didn't remember him! He respected her unwillingness with a loving pat.

As they walked past me (Nancy), I heard the older child confide, "Oh, Daddy! You were gone *so* long and we missed you *so* much!" It was then that I read the word printed on the back of his jacket: NAVY.

It brought back memories of this same scenario when my father was in the Air Force years ago. I was seven years old and the older sister. I hadn't seen him for almost two years. My younger sister, born shortly after Dad's departure, had never laid eyes on him.

What could keep men who obviously adored their families away from their loved ones for months, even years? Like the stranger in the airport and my own beloved father, when you serve your country in the military, you submit to those in authority over you. If this were not so, our country would become unprotected quickly. We would eventually be taken over by a country whose soldiers *were* compliant. At the very core of our freedom is the principle of *submission to authority.*

## A PRINCIPLE IN EVERYDAY LIFE

Perhaps you've never thought about it, but this principle is at work all around you in everyday life. It is the way governments and businesses are run, and it's necessary for maintaining order.

Suppose you went to a fast-food restaurant and everyone wanted to work the counters, but no one was willing to prepare the food. What would it be like if you went to the grocery store and because all the employees wanted to be assigned to the bakery that day, no one stocked the shelves or checked your items at the register? Schools would close if all teachers decided that being a physical education instructor was more fun than teaching English or math. The children might become trained athletes, but they never would learn to read or write.

Can you imagine what life would be like without this underlying principle of authority? It would be chaotic, nonfunctional, and in some cases, life threatening. In the military, this authority is outlined in governmental operating procedures. In the business world, it is delineated by corporate guidelines. In the home, it is declared by the Word of God.

## DECLARED BY THE WORD OF GOD

When you get married, one of your wedding gifts from God is an umbrella which He gives you for protection. It has a name: *submission*. How do we know this was given by God? Because He tells us so in His word:

> Wives, submit to your husbands as to the Lord. (Ephisians 5:22, NIV)

This principle in marriage is often skipped, laughed at, and scorned. It is ignored and derided much to the detriment of the woman it was meant to bless. To most women, there is no flag so red as the flag of submission.

## Submission Defined

Just what does submission mean? If you ask a dozen people, chances are you'll get a dozen answers. Here is a simple definition:

Submission is *voluntarily cooperating with another out of love and respect for God and for that person.*[1]

Perhaps this definition will change your view of submission, as it did for one woman. She said, "Hey, I can do that...I *want* to do that. I don't want not to do that!" Double negative aside, this woman caught a glimmer of God's best for her and said, "I can do it." She said later that her previous failures had occurred because she had left God out of the equation.

*Submission is not an issue of superiority.*

Have you done this, too? If you have, no wonder you're struggling! Leaving God out of the equation is like going deep-sea diving without an oxygen tank. You'd be so busy bobbing to the top for air that you'd never discover the treasures on the ocean floor.

Did you notice that the definition of submission didn't include the words *inferior to* or *less than?* Frequently, these words are interwoven with our idea of what submission means. But this is wrong thinking! The wife isn't inferior to her husband in any way. We are told in Genesis that both are created equally in God's image (Genesis 1:27).

This is reiterated in the New Testament.

There is [now no distinction]...there is not male and female; for you are all one in Christ Jesus. (Galatians 3:28, AMP)

132

## The Chain of Authority

Submission is not an issue of superiority. There is no differentiation in the body of Christ so far as spiritual privilege and position are concerned. However, Paul clearly states that there is headship of the man over the woman.

> Now I want you to realize that the head of every man is Christ, and the head of the woman is man, and the head of Christ is God. (1 Corinthians 11:3, NIV)

We are under our husband's authority—and ultimately God's. Submission is not a demeaning thing.

This is a hard concept to grasp. We're equal to our husbands, yet we're still under their authority. Being under someone simply means that you have less authority than they do—*not* that you're worth less than they are. This in itself is a problem for many women, because we like being the authorities, don't we? Or at least the coauthorities. Yet God, in His infinite wisdom, decided to place a woman not under every man's authority, but under her own husband's authority.

Paul goes on to tell us that "neither was man created for woman, but woman for man" (1 Corinthians 11:9 NIV). This is also a difficult thing for many women to swallow. But here again, this is God's plan. As we said in chapter 1, God didn't consider creation complete until He created woman. In no way was she looked upon as second-rate or as an afterthought. Her very existence helped define Adam.

God's intention is not to make you miserable, and He didn't send Jesus to the cross to assure you a second-class citizenship. His death assured your *royal citizenship,* a citizenship in heaven (Philippians 3:20). This *same* love says, "Wives, submit to your husbands."

## In the Home

There is a God-given chain of authority in the home. The husband is under the authority of God, and the wife is under her husband's authority. In a sense, your husband is the president and you are the vice president. Do you find at times that rather than concentrating on the vice presidency, you are eyeing the office of president? Or maybe you have already made a successful takeover bid and appointed yourself to his position.

Imagine that you've just been asked to interview for the job of vice president in a Fortune 500 company. It is a prestigious position, and you will be reporting directly to the president, the owner's son. You go in for the interview and a copy of your job description is given to you to review. Do you ask to see a copy of the president's job description? Of course not! That is none of your concern. What is your concern, though, is your own job description. Do you go into the job thinking that you will take the presidency away from the president? No, you concentrate on your own job. You have no authority to fire the president. This power lies with someone much higher than you.

This example holds true in your marriage as well. What you are to concentrate on is your own job description. You are responsible for your role. Your husband is responsible for his. What if you do your job, but he doesn't do his? That is between him and the Father. God will deal with a disobedient or ungodly husband. Your concern is whether or not you're doing your job well, and you can gauge this by your obedience.

## Submission Requires Strength

Ten years ago, my family and I (Connie) lived by Puget Sound in Tacoma, Washington. One summer day, our neighbors called and said there was a trail they were going to hike. It was supposed to be especially beautiful, and we agreed to go with them. After packing a picnic lunch, we headed out. We drove to the bottom of the trail, got out of our cars, and began the hike. The spot to which we had driven was already high up in the mountains, and we would be climbing even further. It was a gorgeous day. The air was cool and crisp, and the view was majestic. My husband and I took turns carrying our three-month-old daughter in her carrier, and our four-year-old twins scampered along the trail with the other children. As we marched along, we all agreed that this was a day we'd long remember.

After stopping for lunch, we set out again. Before long, we came to the mountain's edge. A suspension bridge loomed before us, connecting the mountain on which we were now standing to another mountain several hundred feet beyond. Below the bridge ran a large, thundering river. Due to the heavy spring rains, it flowed at a furious pace. Its waters hit the rocks with a mighty crash, and the turbulence was so great that we had to raise our voices to be heard. The water turned white as it tumbled over and over itself on its way downstream.

"Shall we go across?" my friend asked the rest of the group, "Or are you ready to go back?"

What a silly question to ask six children and two adventure-some men!

"Go across!" they shouted enthusiastically.

"Go back!" I said. "There's no way I'm going to cross that bridge. It's already swaying all over the place. What do you think will happen when all of us get on it? It could break!"

I am not a water person. I am comfortable in a bathtub, but beyond that, I become nervous. I didn't learn to swim until I took a beginning course in college, and even then I spent most of the time at the bottom of the pool. The thought of crossing that long, wobbly bridge, which appeared to me to be hanging perilously, seemed insane.

"Come on, honey, I'll help you across," my husband offered.

"I'll get on your other side and help," our neighbor said. "We'll go as slowly as you want."

"No, I'll just sit here with the baby and wait until you come back," I said. "You go ahead. I don't mind a bit."

But they wouldn't hear of it. It was all or none. I took a deep breath and said, "Okay, I'll cross." Then I turned to my husband and warned, "Don't you dare pretend to throw me overboard." My husband threw back his head in laughter and agreed.

With one final look at the mountain upon which my feet firmly rested, off we went. The other adults interspersed themselves among the children, and I brought up the rear. They crossed quickly, while I literally inched my way along. I'm sure I looked a bit idiotic going so slowly, but I didn't care. With every grip of the rope, I braced myself for the bridge to give way. After getting our girls safely across, my husband ran back to help me. I was practically on my hands and knees as I stepped off of the bridge. Everyone cheered wildly! I felt as though I had just won a gold medal in the decathlon! We set off on the second leg of the trip, and it was even more beautiful than the first. Had I been unwilling to cross the bridge, I would never have experienced what lay beyond.

Submission in marriage is similar. The first mountain represents those women who refuse, for whatever reason, to submit to their husbands. Guided by their feelings and molded by the mentality of modern times, they feel secure in their footings and see no reason to change.

The other mountain, sparsely inhabited, represents those women who have chosen to be submissive. Their lives are characterized by an overriding sense of peace, even when the storm clouds rumble overheard. This is a rare thing. The only way to get from the first mountain to the second is over a bridge called obedience.

Do you feel that only weak women cross this bridge? That couldn't be further from the truth. Submission is not for the weak-willed or fainthearted. It requires true discipline and supernatural strength.

This could well be one of the most exciting and liberating principles you will ever discover! Regardless of whether your marriage changes or not, *you* will be changed, and it will bring about a closer walk with God. *God blesses obedience.* This cannot be said enough.

*Submission is not for the weak-willed or fainthearted. It requires true discipline and supernatural strength.*

## YOUR OPINION COUNTS

Does this mean a wife cannot appeal her husband's decisions? Definitely not! In my own marriage (Nancy), if I want to do something—let's use visiting my father as an example—and Ray doesn't want me to go at that time, I will appeal to him, presenting my reasons. And in the end, I do what he asks.

This happened not too long ago. I had just come home from a three-day retreat, walked in the door, and was greeting Ray when the phone rang. It was my beloved dad, who wanted me to come to his home in Virginia to care for him after elective surgery. I thought surely Ray would agree, but he didn't. I expressed my surprise at his decision and expressed my strong desire to go. He explained that I had just returned home, that he didn't mind if I went the following week, but that he wanted to be with me. After all, he reasoned, it was elective and not emergency surgery. The outcome was that I stayed home. This was very difficult, and I was not happy about it, but I privately forgave him. My sister did go, however. She told me later that it meant the world to her and that she and Dad had bonded in a way they had not before—and Dad is eighty-nine and she is fifty-five! This unexpected outcome thrilled me.

## THE HUSBAND'S LEADERSHIP

How can you get your husband to be the leader in your home? Simply put, you can't. *He already is the leader.* God made that clear in the Garden. But you can help your husband assume the leadership role. You do this by introducing into your marriage the things God tells you to do in His Word. When you do, the results can be far-reaching.

Although he has the authority to do so, the husband doesn't necessarily make all the decisions. A wise man sees his wife's giftedness in certain areas and delegates those responsibilities to her.

Certainly, though, if the husband wants things one way and the wife another, the husband is to make the final decision. What if he's dead wrong, as can often be the case? This is often the way he learns the wisdom of considering more carefully his wife's opinion in the future. If she insists on her own way, however, she sows contentiousness and reaps bitterness and division.

One of the privileges of submission is that a woman no longer takes the consequences of a decision upon herself. When she submits to her husband and allows him to lead, the consequences fall on him.

## SUBMISSION'S FRUIT

Submitting to our husbands out of obedience to God's Word is all the motive we need, yet Peter tells us that there may be another result as well:

> So that, if any of them
> do not believe the word,
> they may be won over without words
> by the behavior of their wives." (1 Peter 3:1, NIV)

Your godly behavior may be used by God to influence your husband for eternal good, whether that means winning him to the Savior or influencing his walk with God. It may happen in a matter of weeks, or it may take years.

### A Husband Who Was Won to the Word
In his book, *Straight Talk*, James Dobson, president and founder of Focus on the Family ministries, gives a beautiful example of this

happening. He talks about his paternal grandfather, R. L. Dobson. Dr. Dobson said his grandfather was a good and moral man, but saw no need for the Christian faith.

This spiritual disinterest placed his grandmother under great pressure. She was a devout Christian who felt she must put God first. Therefore, she accepted the responsibility of introducing her six children to Jesus Christ.

In Dr. Dobson's words:

There were times when my grandfather placed tremendous pressure on my grandmother—not to give up her faith, but to leave him out of it.

He said, "I am a good father and provider, I pay my bills, and I am honest in dealing with my fellow man. That is enough."

His wife replied, "You are a good man, but that is not enough. You should give your heart to God." This he could not comprehend.

My ninety-seven-pound grandmother made no attempt to force her faith on her husband, nor did she treat him disrespectfully. But she quietly continued to pray and fast for the man she loved. For more than forty years she brought this same petition before God on her knees.

Then at sixty-nine years of age, my grandfather suffered a stroke, and for the first time in his life he was desperately ill. One day his young daughter came into his room to clean and straighten. As she walked by his bed, she saw tears in his eyes. No one had ever seen him cry before.

"Daddy, what's wrong?" she asked.

He responded, "Honey, go to the head of the stairs and call your mother."

My grandmother ran to her husband's side and heard him say, "I know I'm going to die and I'm not afraid of death, but it's so dark. There's no way out. I've lived my whole life through and missed the one thing that really matters. Will you pray for me?"

"Will I pray?" exclaimed my grandmother. She had been hoping for that request throughout her adult life. She fell to her knees and the intercessions of forty years seemed to pour out through that bedside prayer. R.L. Dobson gave his heart to God that day in a wonderful way.

During the next two weeks, he asked to see some of the church people whom he had offended and requested their forgiveness. He concluded his personal affairs and then died with a testimony on his lips. Before descending into a coma from which he would never awaken, my grandfather said, "...Now there is a way through the darkness."

The unrelenting prayers of my little grandmother had been answered.[2]

## HOW'S YOUR WALK?

There's a well-known saying that goes something like this:

> *Your talk talks,*
> *And your walk talks,*
> *But your walk talks*
> *More than your talk talks.*

That is what being "won over without words by the behavior of their wives," means. Our husbands are far more likely to respond to Christ if they see something in our lives that draws them to Him who lives in us, as Dr. Dobson's grandfather saw in his grandmother. Had she been a wife who had nagged, cajoled, pleaded, and scolded, *why would her husband want what she had?* Your actions speak far louder than what you say. The results are in God's hands.

## SUBMISSION EXEMPLIFIED

What we believe is expressed in the way we behave.

The way we behave reveals our character.

Our character is determined by the choices we make.

Those choices begin with a decision made in our minds.

And these decisions are activated by our wills.

This is what God sees. He sees not as man sees, for a man looks at the outward appearance, but the Lord looks at the heart (1 Samuel 16:7, NASB).

Out of numerous possibilities we've chosen six qualities of godly women, along with the opposite traits. We've found that the opposite traits closely parallel the excuses many women make regarding their lack of submission in marriage.

### 1. Humility versus Pride

*Love is not proud. (1 Corinthians 13:4)*

Many women lack a willingness to follow God's directive in the area of humility. As they read their Bibles, women see for themselves what it has to say on the matter of submission and often discuss it at length. Yet many still disregard the principle of submission.

Often it is not a lack of understanding that keeps them from submitting, but a proud heart. Many women, after reading the passage, ask, "Why should I? Until he changes, why should I?" Their reasons are genuine, but underneath lurks pride. Frequently a woman filled with pride is stubborn and contentious in her marriage.

Ultimately, when you say "I'm doing my part but he's not doing his," you are boasting. You can make yourself look awfully good when you weigh your efforts against your husband's. But this doesn't change what the Lord has asked of you.

When your child comes to you to tattle on a sibling, do you ever say, "You don't need to worry about that"? This same lesson applies here. It is freeing to realize that we don't have to keep score.

Other common justifications for taking over your husband's role include:

*Your choice to obey God must take precedence over your rationalization for taking over the leadership role in your home.*

"He's not as smart, sensitive, or mature as I am."

"He's not a believer, or as good a Christian, or as biblically literate as I am."

"The Lord has gifted me with a discerning spirit, so I'll make the better decision."

"Leadership is not his forte, but it is mine. Therefore he cannot lead, but I can. I will lead our family because he isn't (or can't, or won't, or does it wrong). I have no other choice."

Your choice here is to obey God, and this must take precedence over your rationalization for taking over the leadership role in your home. There is no way you can do both. A woman may feel that her husband actually *wants* her to lead. Could it be that because his leading never suited her it simply became easier to allow her to lead than to be criticized constantly? The bottom line is this:

God has called your husband to lead.
He has called you
to help your husband succeed
in that role.
Any attempt on your part
to wrestle the leadership role
from your husband
is sin.

There is no way around this truth, even if your husband is a nonbeliever. He is still to be the leader of your home.

In other words, your submission isn't about your husband's behavior. It's about your own. Don't try to convince yourself otherwise.

If pride is your sin, humbly confess this sin to God. When you humble yourself in the presence of God, *He* will exalt you! (James 4:10).

## 2. Trust versus Fearfulness

*Love...trusts God always.* (1 Corinthians 13, The Message)

It was an awakening for me (Connie) when I realized that submission was really a trust issue: Could I trust God enough to obey His command? Once I understood this, the issue for me was no longer about submitting; it was about trusting God. I was reminded of my dad swimming in the deep end of a swimming pool. He would say often to my youngest sister, who was standing on the deck, "Jump in and I'll catch you." My sister, who couldn't swim, would jump into his arms every time because she trusted him. This example pales compared to how greatly we can trust Jesus Christ.

### 3. Selflessness versus Self-centeredness
*Love cares more for others than self (1 Corinthians 13, The Message)*
Ephesians 5:21 says that we are to submit to one another out of reverence for Christ, but the very next verse specifically instructs women to submit themselves to their husbands *as to the Lord*. Yet many women are intent on running things their way. This is self-centeredness.

An article in the February 21, 1998, edition of the *Omaha World Herald* was entitled, "The Secret to a Happy Marriage? Men Giving In." The piece says that if men want their marriages to last for a long time, the answer is simple: "Just do what your wife says. Go ahead, give in to her."

The article explains that John Gottman of the University of Washington studied 130 newlywed couples for six years in an effort to find ways to predict both marital success and failure. He and his colleagues discovered that those marriages that worked well had one thing in common—the husband was willing to give in to the wife.

*This is in direct opposition to the Word of God.* When you were a little girl, did you ever have a friend come over to play? Surely one of your friends was bossy. You had to do what she wanted, or else she'd go home! Remember how that made you feel? Is that how your husband feels?

Submitting to your husband displays not only your love for him, but your love for God as well. It is foundational for being a helper to your husband.

### 4. Integrity versus Manipulation

*Love...doesn't force itself on others.* (1 Corinthins 13, The Message)
Do you know how to get the leadership position in your home? Sure you do! We all do! Tears, silence, pouting, harboring grudges, withholding sex, snide remarks, tantrums, and guilt, to name a few. This is called manipulation and is the tool women use most often in holding on to or striving for the leadership role.

Manipulation means to control another by artful, unfair, or insidious means *for your own advantage*. Proverbs 11:1 says that the Lord *abhors* dishonest scales. Doesn't this inspire you to want to avoid manipulation and be a woman of integrity?

Are you a manipulative woman? Is there a power struggle going on in your home? Are you playing tug-of-war with your husband as to who will assume the leadership position? There was a time when that was true in my life (Nancy), and it didn't last for just a short period either. It was a twenty-three-year power struggle, and it occurred because I lacked wisdom.

### 5. Wisdom versus Ignorance

*Love...takes pleasure in the flowering of the truth.*
(1 Corinthians 13, The Message)
In my ignorance, I didn't understand fully what was happening. I was married for twenty-one years before I owned a Bible. I didn't

know what God expected of me as a wife. After receiving Christ as my Savior in 1981 and learning God's principles for marriage, I was shocked. I had thought I was nearly perfect. My parents thought so, as did my teachers in school. And most importantly, I agreed with them completely! How arrogant I was. "If only my husband would change," I thought, "how happy I would be." But the more I got into God's Word, the more convicted I became. *I need to change, Lord, and by Your grace, I will.*

*Manipulation is the tool women use most often in holding on to or striving for the leadership role.*

I realized I had been self-centered, manipulative, and unforgiving. I pored over the marriage verses in Scripture, and one by one, without announcing what I was doing, incorporated them into my life. In the beginning, when I was still immature, I didn't think my husband deserved this. Isn't that an awful way to start? But I wanted to please God, and so I began.

Will *you*?

## 6. Surrender versus Control

*Love…does not demand its own way.*
*(1 Corinthians 13, The Message)*

Maybe you are like the woman who told her friend, "I want to obey Christ, but no matter how hard I try, submission just isn't my spiritual gift." Submission is not a spiritual gift. It is a choice! As one woman told us, "My husband insists that when I say I want him to be the leader in our home, what I really want is to hear *my* words coming out of *his* mouth."

Does this define your attitude toward leadership in the home? Ultimately the whole subject of submission boils down to one issue—control. Letting go of control in the home is a difficult thing for most women. Until you're willing to let go of this, you're missing out on God's plan for your life.

I (Connie) have a wonderful friend named Sandy who is the busy mother of five boys. Just short of her twenty-fifth anniversary, her husband Mike was near death after a three-month bout with cancer. The night before he died, a small group of friends gathered with Sandy at his bedside. We sang, prayed, read Scripture, and reminisced. Sandy shared a story that most of us had never heard. She told how several years earlier, their family had gone to Mexico to share the gospel. They had a great love for the Mexican people and went there annually. Their boys, which included two sets of twins, were seven and younger at the time.

They had been in Mexico for several days and were scheduled to leave the following day. Sandy was feeling sick, as were some of the boys, and she was more than ready to get back to the comforts of her own home. Their plans were to take a bus out the following evening.

"Can't we leave earlier in the day and not wait until evening?" Sandy asked Mike.

"No," Mike said, "I don't think we should leave before evening."

Sandy asked again, but Mike remained insistent, saying, "I feel strongly that we should leave in the evening."

"Okay, you're in charge. I'll go along with your wishes," Sandy replied.

As she told us later, "I had lived my life trying to be a submissive wife, so I felt the final decision was up to him.

"We got on the bus about 7:00 that night. We drove all night, and at about 4:00 the next morning, the bus came to a sudden stop. The passengers woke up, alarmed. We were nowhere near our destination. The driver had gotten a brief radio message that there had been a bad accident and that we could go no further. He knew no details.

"It was only later that we found out that Hurricane Gilberto had wreaked havoc farther up the road we were traveling. A main bridge had been hit and had disappeared into the river below. The morning bus, which I had wanted to take so badly, was en route and received no warning of the impending danger. The driver had no time to react as the bus topped the hill. It plunged into the roaring river below. Everyone on the bus died. Five policemen were killed trying to save some of the people. Had I insisted that we leave earlier, our lives would have been lost as well. My own. My husband's. Our five boys'. I feel the Lord used Mike to spare us."

"He used you, too," we told her. She was oblivious to what we meant. "You could have insisted upon leaving. You were sick, as were the boys. Undoubtedly, you could have worn Mike down and convinced him to leave earlier. But you didn't, because you wanted to submit to his leadership."

Perhaps you're thinking, "But what if it had been the other way around, and the evening bus had crashed instead?" The result would seem tragic. We asked Sandy this very thing, and her response was, "Well, then we would have been in heaven with Jesus. I feel I would have done the right thing even then. We can't always understand the circumstances, but we can always trust Him."

It is impossible to analyze every angle of every situation before deciding to submit to one's husband. What is possible, though, is to obey God's Word and trust Him for the outcome.

## "I'll Do My Part When..."

As we've talked to women over the past few years, we've found that the most common excuse for not carrying out God's role in their marriages is: "I'll do my part when he does his." At the root of this statement lies disobedience.

Whether your husband is doing his part or not has absolutely nothing to do with your obedience to God. Perhaps you hold to the verse in Ephesians 5:21 that says we're to submit to one another out of reverence for Christ. Ideally, this is true—a Spirit-filled person would be sensitive to others' needs and willingly serve them. There would be no domination or self-promotion. This is true for both men and women, but the husband's headship, as determined by God in the Garden, remains intact regardless of whether he chooses this behavior or not.

This verse, however, in no way negates the following verse: "Wives, submit to your husbands as to the Lord." The latter doesn't depend on the former, as many would like to think. Wives are directed specifically to submit, even though their husbands may not treat them in the same considerate manner. A husband's failure to obey verse 21 doesn't excuse or justify a wife's disobedience of verse 22. (Note: There are moral limits to this submission; it is only *as is fitting in the Lord*. A wife is not obligated to follow her husband's leadership if it conflicts with specific scriptural commands.[3] See "Exceptions" in the latter part of this chapter.)

Not to obey what you know to be God's command is disobedience. It is willful rebellion—the very thing that was so costly to Eve.

The only way to successfully submit, and bring glory to Christ as you do, is for your motive to be personal obedience to God's Word. There is no getting around this. Your success is determined by your desire to obey Christ.


## A Final Caution

One last caution: Don't be tempted to use submission to veil what in reality is a cunning, resistant heart. To do so is deceitful. For example, let's say your husband is interviewing for a job in another town. You are happy where you are and don't want to leave the comfortable lifestyle you've carved out for yourself and your family. Perhaps this job is a promotion for your husband, or maybe it would simply cut his commute time in half. You have no intention of moving, but you know it should appear as if the decision were his. So when he asks you what you think, you assure him that you will do whatever he decides.

In the meantime, though, you mention frequently how happy the children are at youth group and how the transition to a new one could be difficult for them. You throw in the names of friends whose children refuse to go to their own youth group to drive home your point. The next day, you say how much you appreciate your local school system and what a wonderful thing it is that your children have found their niches—especially Susie, who struggled so hard before finding hers. You go on to mention that you don't know how she'll adapt to a new school, but probably she'll be okay. If you're lucky. At another time, you wonder aloud who will provide the Christian influence in your neighborhood if your husband takes the new job.

Do you see what's happening? In the end, your husband may think he made the decision, but you know better. *It's perfectly legitimate to discuss worries and concerns, but discuss them outright and without ulterior motives.* Don't throw up a sham of being submissive when you know in your heart that you're not. It can be tempting to do this, yet regardless of who else may be fooled, the Lord is not.

*Don't throw up a sham of being submissive when you know in your heart that you're not.*

We can sometimes become shortsighted and lose perspective. We forget that life isn't just about the here and now, and often we strive to get our way in the smallest of matters. In reality, *all that really matters* is our obedience to God.

Think again about how our obedience brings glory and honor to Jesus. Become awed all over again as you are reminded that you have something to offer Him. Think as well about how you want to be used by God. You don't want anything to hinder this. Our passion is to be used mightily for His kingdom. What a privilege! Yet we can prevent His using us when we disobey. We want the door to be wide open—not just mostly open or open most of the time.

## SEVEN SIMPLE TIPS

Many times what is pleasing to God is seen as foolishness by the world. Certainly this is the case regarding submission. We've listed seven simple tips that will help you go against the flow in this area.

1. Ask the Lord to give your husband wisdom and discernment.

2. Raise the level of your expectations of God's power working in your husband's life. Have you put a limit on your expectations of what God can do?

3. Make a conscious effort to listen to your husband's point of view without a quick rejection.

4. Begin to ask your children to seek their father's permission and counsel. My (Nancy) children initially asked, "Why? We've not done this before." Even he questioned me, it was so far from the norm.

5. Affirm him when he makes a wise decision. Tell him how you saw the wisdom in what he did. It is so often true that a person rises to the level of another's trust in him.

6. Pray for your own obedience.

7. When you and your husband disagree on an issue, even after talking it over, it is often a struggle to surrender your viewpoint. When his decisions prove to be wise, complement him and express your confidence in his leadership. When he is wrong, as he sometimes will be, be gracious. Your attitude could well begin to build his respect for *your* wisdom.

## EXCEPTIONS

You might be wondering whether there are exceptions in the area of submission. There are. God is the highest authority, and anything that goes against His Word should not be done. You are called first to submit to God's authority and then to your husband's. If submitting to your husband's authority violates God's teachings, then your choice must be to obey God, not your husband. Some of the exceptions are crystal clear: adultery, abuse, asking you to worship other gods. There are many other areas, however, that aren't as clear, and women wonder what they are to do in these cases. If you have such questions, or if your husband is asking you to do something illegal or immoral, you should take action. We suggest you:

1. Seek counsel from God.
2. Prayerfully appeal to your husband.
3. Seek counsel from your pastor or other church leader whom you trust.

## SUBMISSION IN THE GODHEAD

Submission is seen supremely in the Godhead: The head of Christ is God. Look again at 1 Corinthians 11:3, NIV:

> Now I want you to realize that the head of
> every man is Christ, and the head of the woman
> is man, and the head of Christ is God.

Jesus Himself, who is equal with His Father, submitted to His Father's will completely. In fact, He said, "My food is to do the will of Him who sent me and to accomplish His work" (John 4:34, NASB). Regarding His will, He said, "I do not seek My own will but the will of Him who sent Me" (John 5:30, NASB).

Isn't this the way you want to live your life? Is your food to do the will of God? Do you desire to accomplish His work? Then choose to submit all areas of your life to Him, as Jesus did, including submission to your husband.

Which do you think required more strength? To do His Father's will, or His own? Was He *weak* or *strong* when He:

> gave up His glory to come to earth as a baby?
> gave up His voice, choosing to simply cry as a newborn?
> allowed Himself to be wrapped in swaddling clothes, unable to walk, carried along by Mary and Joseph?

Did he exhibit *strength* or *weakness* when He agreed to:

> be subject to His earthly parents?
> be seized by human hands, mocked, spat upon, slapped, and scourged?
> go willingly to the cross, knowing the pain He would endure?
> refuse the tauntings to come down off the cross and prove Himself God?
> endure the silence of His own Father when He became sin for the world?
> place His own desires behind those of His Father?

Submission isn't a position of weakness, but strength. It is the key to a wholehearted commitment to God's Word and to becoming the wife God meant for you to become.

## CHAPTER 5 SUMMARY

1. We are to submit first to Jesus as Lord of our lives, and then to our husbands.

2. Obedience to God's Word is the motivation for submission.

3. Through her actions, a godly wife may change a disobedient husband's ways.

4. God, in His infinite wisdom, decided to place a woman not under every man's authority, but under her own husband's authority.

5. The power to submit comes from Jesus Christ working in you as you obey His Word.

6. The only exception to submitting to your husband is if it causes you to violate God's will.

7. Don't attempt to use submission to mask a stubborn, resistant heart.


8. The Savior is calling you to obedience. Will you heed His call?

In 1986 one of the largest diamonds ever unearthed was found in the Premier Mine in Transvaal, South Africa. Weighing 755.50 carats, it displayed the color of a bright red rose at its core, changing to a golden yellow on the outer surfaces. Nothing like this had been seen before, and De Beers, the owner of the stone, turned to a master cutter for guidance. A team was assembled to cut the stone.

The preparations were amazing! An underground bunker was built so that there would be no vibrations as the gemologists worked. Great care was taken to see that the atmosphere was calm and peaceful. The walls were even painted a pale green to keep the eyes relaxed. The tools used were carefully made of dull metals, so that the only shining object would be the stone itself. The entire process took three years, and when finished, the diamond weighed 545.67 carats. It was bought by a group of businessmen from Thailand as a gift for their king on the fiftieth anniversary of his reign.

Did you know that the Bible says that there is something worth far more than jewels; something with which a 545-carat diamond cannot compare? It is a godly wife. She is precious in God's sight and is considered of great value to Him.

Are you a godly wife? Do you desire to become one? You can! Do you feel inept, unqualified, or just not up to it? God understands your feelings, your doubts, your fears. He also knows your heart, and can work mightily in one that's yielded to Him. You are a diamond—a diamond in the rough—a diamond in the making. Place yourself into the hands of the Master Jeweler, Jesus Christ. Allow Him to chisel you, mold you, and refine you into the kind of wife that reflects His glory.

*An excellent wife—she is worth far more than jewels!*

# CHAPTER SIX

# Godly Behavior

*Godly behavior is a jewel that
expresses the radiance of Christ.*

I've got a question for you," a seminar speaker recently announced to a large group of married women. "Raise your hand if you think it's important to be a good wife to your husband." Everyone in the group raised her hand. The speaker continued, "Now raise your hand if you consider yourself a good wife." Far fewer hands were raised. "How many of you feel you were a good wife at some point in your marriage but have gotten off track along the way?" The majority of women raised their hands. "My last question," the speaker said, "is to ask how many of you would be willing to find out what God has to say about being a godly wife and would then be willing to put those principles into practice if you knew what they were?" Hand after hand after hand was raised. A sense of excitement and anticipation filled the room.

Such was the scene recently as women met to discover just what it means to be a godly wife. Dozens of women came the first week. More came the second week, as women brought their friends. And even more came on the third week. The room was full and getting fuller. The word was out: marriages could be changed. And the changes began when these women started to grasp what their God-given job descriptions were as wives.

Why do we feel it is of utmost importance to be a godly wife, yet so few of us feel that we are? For both of us, it was because we had no idea what our job description was for wives. Prior to that time our focus in our marriage had been wrong as had been our motives for doing things.

In this chapter, you will begin to see what your job description is as a wife. A job is so much easier to do if you know what you're supposed to be doing. I (Connie) recently asked one of my daughters to clean the bathroom. She cleaned it and was finished in an amazingly short amount of time.

"Did you clean it thoroughly?" I asked.

"Yes," she said.

A while later I went in and looked it over. On the surface, it appeared clean. But as I looked closer, there were areas that hadn't been touched. I brought this to my daughter's attention.

"I didn't know to clean in those places, Mom. You've never really shown me how to clean the bathroom. You just tell me to clean it."

My daughter was right. She was doing the best job that she

could with the knowledge that she had. I later taught her how to clean a bathroom thoroughly, and she's been doing so ever since.

That's often how it is for us in our roles as wives. We fall short, not because we want to, but because we don't know exactly what we're supposed to be doing. Hopefully, after reading this chapter, your job description will be clearer, and you will feel a renewed sense of purpose and joy in your role as a wife.

## OBSERVABLE TRAITS

Peter spoke specifically of *purity* and *reverence* in marriage:

> When they observe
> the pure and modest way
> in which you conduct yourself,
> together with your reverence. (1 Peter 3:2, AMP)

We are going to examine these two observable traits. We want you to be mindful that as we express ways we've responded to our husbands, the Holy Spirit will direct you how to act and respond to your own husband.

### Purity

> Purity: to refrain from acts, thoughts, or desires that are not sanctioned by the marriage vows. To be modest in deportment and dress as the outward sign of inward purity.

As is evident in this definition, purity is something inward as well as outward, involving both our thoughts and actions.

### Our Thoughts

We see from David's life that adultery begins in the thought life. David saw Bathsheba bathing. He *thought* about her, sent for her, conceived a child with her, and ordered her husband to the front lines in battle, knowing he would be killed (2 Samuel 11). We see that David, "a man after God's own heart," struggled with his thought life, and it led to a serious breach of conduct.

You can't always choose the thoughts that come into your mind, but you can decide whether you will think on them. If there's something on television that you don't want to watch, what do you do? You either change the channel or turn off the TV. Do the same thing in your thought life. The moment a thought comes into your mind that is not pure—maybe it's a past relationship or a man you find yourself admiring—banish it! Start thinking about something else. Philippians 4:8 says to think on things that are true, noble, right, pure, lovely, and admirable. If your thoughts don't fall into these categories, switch the channel.

> *You can't always choose the thoughts that come into your mind, but you can decide whether you will think on them.*

A woman may find herself thinking about or admiring other men while her own husband goes weeks without a single word of admiration or encouragement from her. Find things in your *husband* that you appreciate and then verbally acknowledge them. You'll be surprised at what a difference it makes in both your lives.

### Our Eyes

Choose wisely what you watch on TV and at the movies. Many women admit to letting the lines blur in this regard. Watch how you speak and what you read. Many novels set up an unrealistic idea of what your life should be like. Women's magazines do this as well.

### Our Dress

Take care in how you dress; seductive clothing is for your bedroom. Just as you want to protect your own thought life, you don't want to dress in a manner that will cause a man to struggle. A male friend at our church said recently, "I find it surprising how often I have to consciously choose to look away from how a woman is dressed, even at church. And I'm not talking about how the teenage girls are dressing. I'm talking about women in their thirties, forties, and fifties."

### Matters of Privacy

Respect each other's privacy in the bathroom at toilet time. Knock before entering, and request your husband to do the same. Some women feel it's an indication of a good relationship when they and their husbands can share the rest room when one of them is using the toilet. However, it remains our belief that that time should be kept personal and private, since neither of you is being at your best then.

### Reverence

You are to feel for him all that reverence includes—to respect, defer to, revere him; (revere means) to honor, esteem, (appreciate, prize), and (in the human sense) adore him; (and adore means) to admire, praise, be devoted to, deeply love and enjoy (your husband).[1]

Reverence is honor or respect, felt or shown. We will see that reverence has many aspects and we will address several of them here.

### Reverence: To Respect

Respect: the special esteem or consideration in which one holds another person or thing.[2]

Survey after survey tells us that a woman's greatest desire in marriage is to feel loved by her husband, while a man's number one desire is to be respected by his wife. Respect must be one of the more difficult traits for wives to exhibit because not only does Peter mention it, Paul does as well.

And the wife must see to it that she respects her husband. (Ephesians 5:33, NASB)

A wife's respect is shown by highly regarding her husband. Often women withhold respect from their husbands, feeling that their husbands don't deserve it. "When he starts doing such and so," many women say, "then I'll give him my respect."

When a woman does this, what she is doing is *rewriting the Bible*. Notice that it doesn't say, "Wives, see to it that you respect your husbands *if* they deserve it." It says, "Wives, see to it that you respect your husbands." It is a directive to wives. They must choose whether they will respect their husbands. Do you respect your husband conditionally? Do you manipulate him to do certain things before you give him your respect? Are you still waiting for him to change, thinking that then you will respect him? Remember, respect is not something your husband must earn from you. It is something you must give him because of the role God gave him—husband.

A practical way to demonstrate respect is by giving particular attention to your husband. Practice something that is becoming more and more rare in these fast-paced days in which we live: the fine art of listening.

### A Lost Art

In our busy world, it seems that everyone is talking and no one is listening. But you can learn to develop your listening skills. Your objective is to draw the talker out, keeping attention away from yourself and on the other person.

"I had an interesting phone call today," says your husband.

Which response might draw him out?

1. "Tell me about it...."

2. "So did I. My mother called and said...."

Obviously, the first choice is correct. When you ask him to tell you about it, stop what you are doing, and look at him as he tells you about the call.

Perhaps he might say, "My cousin called, and my high school wants to nominate me as a candidate for their Hall of Fame. They need information about my life and achievements."

This could lead to an evening of happy reflection, with both of you thinking of things to put in his letter. The key is to keep the focus on him if you want a husband who communicates. You can share some of the events of your day a bit later as he basks in the glow of knowing "my wife cares about me!"

### Seven Ways to Better Listening

Here are seven additional tips to enhance your listening skills.

**1. Look at your husband when he speaks to you.**

If your eyes are focused elsewhere, it will appear that your mind is as well. Stop whatever it is you are doing and look at your husband as he speaks.

**2. Lean forward as you listen.**

Being on the "edge of your seat," with your body bent towards him as he speaks, shows him that you are more than just being kind, you are very interested in what he is saying.

**3. Give feedback.**

Respond to his words by nodding and smiling. Ask questions. This lets him know that you were listening closely to what was said.

**4. Don't interrupt or change the subject.**

Wives are renowned for this! Let your husband finish his own sentences, and allow him to finish talking about the subject he's discussing, even if it's not your favorite. Don't yawn, look at your watch, or glance around the room or out the door or window.

**5. Repeat back to him some of the things he said.**

This shows you were listening and is validating and confirming.

**6. Compliment him on his insights and wisdom.**

This will encourage him to continue sharing with you in the future.

### 7. Show your appreciation.

Thank him for sharing his thoughts with you. Men are wired differently and often don't realize how much it means to a woman for her husband to talk to her.

A friend told us how one Christmas Eve, because of the relaxed work schedule, her husband spent an afternoon in the kitchen talking with her. They talked about the past year and discussed hopes and plans for the coming New Year. She later told him that this time was the best gift he had ever given her. He was taken aback. "Little did I realize how much this meant to my wife, and her expressing her thanks made me want to do it more often."

### Reverence: To Defer

Defer: allowing someone else's opinion and judgment to have more weight than one's own, willingly or politely.[3]

My sister Christine and I (Nancy) visit each other several times a year. It is delightful to spend time with her in Dallas. One of our favorite things to do is browse through the wonderful specialty stores near her home. On one such trip, Christine found a colorful rag rug for her kitchen. We both agreed it would fit perfectly and matched the shades of color in her kitchen.

We were right. It couldn't have looked more charming. We both loved the way it looked and couldn't wait to show it to Christine's husband.

When he came home that evening, he immediately told her that he couldn't stand the rug. He said that it reminded him of his childhood poverty and the rugs his mother made from scraps because she could afford nothing better.

My sister gave me an unforgettable lesson in deference at this point. She simply said, "Well, darling, I'll take it back." Instead of a war of wills, instead of hurt feelings, Christine weighed the situation. She demonstrated that a small rug is of little importance to her, whereas her relationship with her husband is vital.

### Practical Ideas

Below are some other practical ways that a wife can defer to her husband.

### 1. Financial

One woman fought for years with her husband over how to invest their money. She liked the idea of insured deposits, while he liked the idea of the stock market. The very thought of owning stocks made her cringe. It quickly became a sore spot between them. He resented her controlling ways. She resented his recklessness, as she saw it. After being taught about deference in marriage, she chose to defer to her husband in this area, even though her mind remained unchanged regarding the investments. Although the stock market was often volatile, the atmosphere in the home no longer was. As she deferred to her husband, he frequently came to ask her opinion on things. At one point, he volunteered to keep as much in insured accounts as he did in the stock market, all because she had chosen to defer to him. This is *not* to say that your finances will improve if you defer to your husband. If he's a poor money manager, you may lose money. Maybe living on your present income is a struggle, and you feel your husband is unwise in his spending. What do you do? You can appeal to him and give your input, but he alone is answerable to God for how he does things. Allow the final decision to be his, and leave the results between him and God.

## 2. Messy versus Tidy

Many wives struggle with husbands who are messy. These women come to resent the dropped clothing, the dirty socks, the tools that are left lying hither and yon. One woman told of such a situation in her home. She sought help from an older woman in the church. "How much time would it take you if you picked up these things for your husband?" the woman asked.

The wife replied, "Probably five or ten minutes a day."

"Wouldn't it be time well spent if you chose to serve your husband in this way instead of letting it eat away at you day after day?"

There are a few women who struggle with the opposite problem: husbands who are extremely tidy and fastidious. These women can choose to defer to their husbands by making a point of cheerfully keeping their things picked up and teaching their kids to do the same.

## 3. Personal Preferences

Most men, when asked, have opinions on things. Are we willing to respect these opinions when they are different than ours? This is a practical area in which you can defer to your husband, and one he will appreciate.

A few years ago during the holidays, my (Connie) husband and I were in a large department store and passed a clearance aisle as we left. We saw some tiny demitasse cups that I thought would be perfect for our three daughters, as they enjoy having tea parties. The regular price for a set of four was eighteen dollars. However, the set was marked down to two dollars.

"Let's get them for the girls," I said to my husband.

"Let's not," he responded, "I don't like those large orange splotches in the middle of each cup."

"Me, neither," I said, "but for two dollars, I don't mind them so much."

"There's no reason to spend two dollars on something you don't really like," he reasoned, "even if it is a good deal."

He was talking to the queen of bargains, and I wanted to pressure him into buying the cups. My daughters hadn't ask for cups like these, and I'd never once thought of buying any before. We had managed well with what we had at home, but the incredible markdown convinced me that *we needed those cups*. However, my husband disagreed. So I consciously chose to defer to my husband, although every bargain-hunting bone in my body disagreed with him. Amazingly, two weeks later we were in the same store. My husband, who is not normally a bargain shopper, ventured over to the clearance aisle. There were some demitasse cups that weren't there before. They, too, were marked down to two dollars. They were elegant and beautiful—not a single orange splotch on them! We bought them, but even better than the bargain was knowing that I had chosen to defer to my husband's wishes.

### Deferring to an Unwise Husband

There are times when a wife is put in the position of having to defer to an unwise husband. How should she handle this? She can make suggestions that are well reasoned and openly discuss what she feels the ramifications might be. We personally share our opinions with our husbands, and through the years, as we have grown in wisdom, our husbands have often asked for our opinions and followed our suggestions, but not always. We strive to accept their leadership and decisions.

If it is immoral or goes against the teachings of God, a woman is not to defer to her husband. Her ultimate deference must be to Him. But if immorality or disobedience to God's law is not involved, then a woman should choose to defer to her husband. The bottom line is this: Your husband is responsible before God for his decisions—good or bad—and you have the protection of being in the will of God when you defer to him.

### Reverence: To Revere

Revere: to regard with affectionate awe or veneration.[4]

One of the keepsakes that I (Nancy) have from my mother is a big bowl she received from the Jewel Tea Company years ago. I still remember that Mom's potato salad was served from it when I was a little girl. It has a few chips in it, but that doesn't diminish my regard for it. I still use it several times a month. I treat it with enormous care, making sure to take it out of the cabinet with two hands so it won't drop. Extra care is taken when I wash it and place it back on the shelf. Each time I use it, I think of my mother and of the deep love that we shared.

I revered my mother. I regarded her with great love and affection, and I respected her deeply. It is a wonderful thing to revere a parent, but the Bible tells us that there is someone else worthy of reverence: your husband.

Your husband is a man of great value to God. Jesus died for him and yearns to bring him into a right relationship with Himself. God has given him a special name: husband. Not to revere his

God-given title is to damage your marriage. Marriage is God's idea, and He considers your relationship with your husband as sacred and valuable.

### How Long Has It Been?

How long has it been since you have revered your husband? If you're like most women today, the dailyness of life has a way of taking its toll, and it has probably been far too long. Too often we are left wondering why we ever held them in awe in the first place.

Would you be willing to revere your husband once again? You may feel inadequate to do so or that your husband is undeserving of your reverence. Don't worry! Be faithful in your attempt to introduce this concept into your marriage. God will bless your efforts as you begin afresh to revere your husband and the position of leadership in which he's been placed.

### Regaining the Awe

There are many ways you can begin to demonstrate to your husband that you revere him. If you're feeling stretched, that's good news! It shows that you're willing to change. We felt the same way, as years had gone by in our marriages without our doing this. Once we began, however, we wondered why we hadn't begun sooner. As we chose obedience by revering our husbands, we felt uplifted ourselves by the Lord for doing so.

Are you feeling like you need some help to get you started? You might consider some of the following ideas:

- Regard him as worthy of great honor in the way you speak of him and talk to him. This is especially important before others: your children, his and your parents, friends, coworkers.

- Look at him with softness. There are times when my (Connie) husband has told me that he dislikes it when I look at him "that way" or give him "the look." A simple thing as how we look at our husbands conveys volumes about our thoughts about them.

- Try making your phone calls when he isn't home, and take only emergency calls when he's home. I (Nancy) made a point of doing this years ago, and my husband appreciates it immensely. If a friend calls in the evening, I politely tell her that my husband is home and ask if I could call her back at a later time. Friends have said that though they thought this quite odd in the beginning, they now do the same thing, and their husbands have expressed appreciation that they no longer spend much of the evening on the phone.

- Consistently prepare something he likes for dinner and serve him the choicest portion. Too often the kids receive this serving, and dad chooses from what's left. When we began doing this, our children loved it. They greatly enjoyed seeing us treat their fathers in this way.

### Reverence: To Honor

Honor: to treat with respect, honor, regard; one whose worth brings respect.[5]

Over forty years ago, at Fuchu Air Force Base in Tokyo, Japan, I (Nancy) was the secretary who recorded the testimony at the court martial of a sergeant. The charge against him was that he didn't maintain order in his home. In reality, it was his wife who did not tend her home and children when her husband was at work. By all accounts, when the sergeant was at home, things ran smoothly. Tragically, he was reduced in rank and had to leave the Air Force because his lowered salary could not support his family.

A wife must maintain her husband's good name, public esteem, and reputation. Not to do so reflects poorly on her husband and in some cases can affect his employment.

### Ways to Honor Your Husband

A wife can honor her husband by:

1. Making sure her own behavior is beyond reproach. A woman's behavior affects how others see her husband.

2. Not dishonoring his name in any way before others. "Husband bashing" has become far too common when women get together. It is easy to join in and even try to one-up each other regarding our husbands' faults. It is one thing to bring your personal problems before a *trusted* Christian counselor, pastor, or friend, and quite another to share your husband's faults with casual or even close friends. Also, be cautious with prayer requests. Not every Christian keeps a confidence. Prayer requests can often wind up as gossip.

3. Remembering that if you are married to a Christian man, you are married to someone of highest worth to Christ. If Christ regards your husband as precious and worthy, how can you possibly not? A woman who is married to a non-Christian should treat her husband in the same way. Christ

died for his sins as well and desires a relationship with him. First Peter 3:1–2 says that our behavior may be the vessel that is used to win a non-Christian husband to Christ. If your husband is a non-Christian, based on your behavior alone would he have any desire to know more about your Savior?

4. Asking yourself whether your children see you honoring their father. You greatly influence how they view their father by how you honor him in your home.

5. Remembering that honor involves all that you do with your life—the way you talk and work, the values you hold, your morals. There is nothing that you do, say, watch, or read that doesn't involve honor.

Are you, as a wife, bringing honor to God in the way you treat your husband? We are to "love each other with brotherly affection and *take delight* in honoring each other" (Romans 12:10, TLB, emphasis added). Are you taking delight in honoring your husband?

### Reverence: To Adore

Adore: (in the human sense) to regard with loving devotion by giving time, effort, and care.[6]

In the last six years of her life, my (Nancy) mother was almost totally restricted to her bedroom because of emphysema. My dad began to sleep on a couch in her room to be near her and tend to her needs. After four years of caregiving, Dad, in his late seventies, needed a bit more help. So he and mom left their home in Texas and moved into ours in North Carolina. There I watched his continual devotion to his beloved Teresa. I could help during the day, but at night he took over all her needs, sleeping on a daybed in her room.

Towards the end, as Mom grew weaker, she couldn't leave her bed. Dad remained her constant companion, placing her as his priority over all else. He oversaw her medication and attended to her oxygen machine. All of this took a toll on my father. He was in his early eighties, and he was aging quickly.

The night Mom died, I remember coming downstairs around midnight and hearing sounds of troubled breathing, as we had heard countless times before. I tiptoed into their room, and there, resting at the foot of her bed, was my faithful father.

This time, as we struggled to help her, we knew the time had come for her to leave behind the trials of this world. With my father sitting with his arms around her, she slipped into the presence of Jesus.

This is devotion. This is adoring, in the human sense. Did Mom appreciate this? Unbelievably, she confided to me that her last years were the happiest of her life! How she loved Dad!

God did the dearest thing for my father. Dad bought the home in which he was born ninety years ago in Virginia. He lives alone, surrounded by pictures of Mom. He plays tennis three times a week and walks several miles a day. He looks years younger than his age. I think it is God saying, "Well done, good and faithful servant."

How devoted are you to your *husband?*

### Not too Late to Begin
One woman we know, after twenty-five years of marriage, decided being devoted to someone other than herself sounded

like a challenge worth trying. She began noticing what her husband liked, what he needed, and what pleased him. He blossomed with all this new attention, and she began loving him in a brand-new way.

Not too long ago, he exuberantly declared, "Coming home to you is like going to a five-star resort. Whenever I sit in my chair at night, I feel like I'm sitting in first class."

Try adoring your husband and see what happens!

Are we getting carried away? Most women find it easy to adore special people and various things. One woman we know said she adored her kids, fun friends, fabulous restaurants, and clothes that made her look like she had a waistline. When asked if she adored her husband, she was shocked!

"Surely you're joking," she said incredulously. "Grown women don't adore their husbands."

"Why not?" we asked.

"I don't know," she said, a bit perplexed. "We just don't. We respect them and love them, but adore them? No, we don't. Furthermore, I'm not sure mine would want to be adored. He'd say that was strictly a feminine thing."

We challenged this woman to go home and ask her husband how he would feel about her adoring him. So she did. Without any explanation, she asked simply, "Do you think you'd like it if I adored you?"

"Absolutely," was his instant reply.

"Are you kidding?" she responded, giving him a chance to rethink his quick answer.

"No, I'm not kidding," he assured her. *"There's not a man I can think of who wouldn't love being adored by his wife."*

### Reverence: To Admire

Admire: To marvel; to wonder; to astonish;
to be delighted by.[7]

To admire your husband is one of the most powerful things you can do for him. It is so potent that you must do it wisely and without manipulation. Most men prefer being admired to being loved. If you doubt this, tell your husband that you love him and study his reaction. Then, after prayerful consideration, think of something you admire about him. Say to him, "There is something about you that I truly admire." Watch his attentiveness. You will be amazed at how powerful words of admiration are to your husband.

### Admiration Can Transform a Marriage

We know of a couple who were in the direst of straits in their marriage. Over the years their love had cooled towards each other. Their children had all left home, and the need for conversation was almost nil. He took care of his needs; she took care of hers. In what should have been their golden years together, they lived in quiet, lonely worlds of their own.

After hearing teaching on the topic of admiring, the wife decided that maybe this was something she could do for her husband. For several nights she tried to get the words out of her mouth, but none came. It was too awkward, too hard, too uncomfortable. Finally one night she put all of her discomfort aside and plunged in. Slowly, hesitantly, she told her husband that she admired the way he had worked hard over the years to put a roof over his family's head. There was an awkward silence. She heard a muffled sound and discovered that her husband was so moved by her words that he was in tears. The walls had begun to come down. She credits her sincere words of admiration as the beginning of a healing that took place in her marriage over the following several years.

Another friend had become so embittered in her marriage that she balked completely in this area. "There is absolutely nothing I admire in him," she said. Finally, after much thinking, she came up with something. "I admire the way he takes care of his personal hygiene," she said. While this may sound like a stretch, she shared it with him. "Believe it or not, he was touched. Touched that I would verbalize anything like that. Touched that I noticed. And touched that I would swallow my pride long enough to share this with him, because my pride is something that's come between us for a long time."

*Most men prefer being admired to being loved.*

Would you consider saying to your husband tonight, "There is something about you I truly admire"? Then share it with him. Lay your discomfort aside. Swallow your pride if you need to. Ask God for a spirit of humility and sincerity. Then step out in faith and tell your husband you admire him. You can do it! And God will bless you in your efforts.

### Focus on His Strengths

Most men appreciate being admired physically. What about his body do you admire? Maybe his brute strength? Maybe his long legs or strong arms? One man we know wears his hair a certain way because his wife has told him how much she likes it. You could admire your husband's lovemaking skills—his gentleness or sensitivity.

Sometimes a woman will consider traits she had once admired in her husband as faults or flaws.

My (Nancy) husband, Ray, is direct, blunt, and to the point. He is honorable and honest. He says what he thinks and means what he says. He doesn't sugarcoat his conversations. It was one of the things about him that attracted me to him. As time passed, however, I began to view his manner of speech as rather rude and unfriendly. Without conscious thought, or his asking or desiring my assistance, I decided to help him overcome this. The stress this effort created in me lasted for years until I realized what I was doing. I began to notice the wise counsel he gave to our children. They might not always appreciate the way he makes his point, but they deeply appreciate his insight, and so do I.

Now I seldom offer advice on how he expresses himself—he doesn't need it. Far too few people say what they think. I once again see this as a strength and admire it in my husband.

### Advice Worth Remembering

A friend who is a counselor once said, "Most frequently it is not a younger woman, or a more beautiful woman, or a thinner woman that captures a married man's attention, but it is an admiring woman. Few women realize just how powerful words of admiration are to a man. Wives would be wise to remember that this is an area in which they can tremendously impact their husbands. If he is admired in his own home, he is much less likely to go looking for it someplace else."

### Reverence: To Praise

Praise: to express approval; to commend.[8]

How good it feels to be praised! We praise our children for learning new skills or bringing home a good paper from school. We praise our friends for losing weight, for hosting a successful luncheon, or for making a difficult decision. We praise our pets for their loyalty and eagerness to please us. We even praise total strangers whom we will most likely never see again. But rare is the woman who praises her husband.

Praise, like admiration, is a powerful thing to a man. Regardless of their temperaments, education, income, or anything else, men desire to hear words of praise from their wives. Too often, the words of praise that overflowed in the relationship in earlier years have turned into words of criticism and harshness.

But the good news is that praise can be reintroduced into a marriage at any time! It is one of the simplest things to do: Here again are some practical tips to get you started.

### Practical Pointers

1. Try noticing the things he does right and let him know that you notice.
2. If he does something for you, don't criticize the way he does it.
3. If he buys you an orange robe for Christmas, resist the urge to immediately ask whether or not he kept the sales receipt.
4. Comment on the yard when he mows it. If he doesn't mow it, don't mention repeatedly that you greatly admire your neighbor, Frank, for mowing his so faithfully.

5. Thank him for filling your car with gasoline, having the oil changed, checking the tires, or anything else he does for you in this regard.

Everyone is different! A dear older friend once said that she was horrified when she called her married daughter and asked what she was doing. "I'm mowing the lawn, Mother," the daughter said.

The mother said, "Why are you mowing the lawn? Shouldn't Bob be doing that?"

"No," the daughter laughed, "I'm mowing the lawn, and he's cooking a fabulous dinner."

Be creative and thoughtful about how you can sincerely praise your husband. Don't make any announcements or make such an issue of it that the attention actually falls onto you.

Also, don't use guilt, manipulation, or nagging to get your husband to do something so that you can praise him. Maybe your husband does very little for you. Frequently, men say they don't do things because their wives will criticize the way they did them. Are you guilty of this? We know of one couple where the husband arranged a getaway weekend as a surprise for his wife. The wife was upset when she discovered that they weren't staying at a certain hotel, and she told him repeatedly of her disappointment. The weekend was ruined for both of them, and her husband stopped thinking of ways to surprise her.

It is generally believed that for every negative statement someone makes, anywhere from seven to ten positive statements are needed to counteract the negative words. Practically put, every time you tell your husband he did something wrong, to offset the negative words you would need seven to ten opportunities to tell him he did something right.

## Changed Through Praise

Very rarely do critical words cause someone to change. Far more effective in causing change are positive words or words of praise. One friend was constantly reminding her husband to take out the trash. He was absentminded and could never quite remember when to take it out. This irritated his wife no end. She was convinced that he could remember if he tried. But week after week, he forgot. And week after week, she complained and criticized. It was during this time that she heard this teaching on praising and expressing approval of one's husband. *Hmm,* she thought to herself. *I wonder if it works.*

Our friend began biting her tongue whenever she was tempted to nag her husband, not only about the trash, but in other areas in which she considered him lacking as well. "After three days, " she said, "I don't think I had any tongue left to bite. I had bitten on it constantly. I was surprised at how frequently, sometimes constantly, I spoke negative words to my husband. I realized that some days it was an all-out assault. I was horrified."

This woman purposed in her heart to change, and with God's help, she did. She made what for her was a huge decision: she decided that she would no longer mention the trash unless it was to thank her husband on those rare days that he remembered to take it out. Several weeks went by, and she found herself taking the trash out. But no longer did she feel anger or hardened as she had prior to that time. "There was a certain sense of joy in taking out the trash. It wasn't the act itself that gave me joy. The joy came in knowing I was taking out the trash as unto the Lord and in knowing this was no longer an issue between my husband and me. God had removed the anger and frustration I had felt for so long. It didn't really matter to me anymore who took out the trash. I started thanking God that I was physically able to do it."

Then one week, without prompting, her husband remembered. She thanked him. A few weeks later, he remembered again. Once again, she humbly and sincerely expressed her appreciation. "Before long," she told us, "he was remembering more than he was forgetting. And on the days that he forgot, he felt badly that he had forgotten, and assured me that he'd try to remember the next time. All because, I believe, I had started using words of praise instead of words of criticism."

If you do this will your husband change, too? Of course there is no way to know. But we do believe that you will change if you decide in your heart to accept your husband as a gift and treat him accordingly.

### Reverence: To Love Deeply

Love Deeply: A profound, powerful emotion
felt for another person.[9]

There is a program on television that chronicles the courtship and marriage of couples. Since marriage is a subject I (Nancy) care deeply about, I have watched it occasionally with much interest and intrigue. I find it fascinating to see why couples choose to marry each other. Without exception, the couples express deep love for each other and freely convey their reasons for marrying. Knowing from statistics that half of these couples will divorce, one can spot the "red flag" statements that could spell trouble as time goes by. One starry-eyed husband said that he loved her because she had never let him down. She loved him because he loved her so much, and she didn't think anyone else in the world would ever love her like that.

What will happen when she lets him down, as she will surely do at some point? Will he love her less, and thus negate the very reason she chose him?

"I love him because he is so handsome, tender, spontaneous, helpful, interesting...."

These lists could go on and on. You can probably recall your own reasons for marriage. The ones we've listed, however, do not define the highest love one person can have for another. That love is holier and stronger. The love you are to have for your husband is the kind that doesn't run out. You don't fall out of true love because you don't fall into true love—*you choose to love.*

Love is a choice you make to be primarily concerned with the well-being of another, regardless of his reaction or condition. This is *agape* love—the love Jesus has for you. Jesus said, "Love one another even as I have loved you.... by this all men will know that you are My disciples" (John 13: 34-35, NASB).

You show this kind of love to your husband by being unselfishly loyal to him. Hold him dear. Respond to his lovemaking. Show him how much he means to you. Not just with words or actions, but with both. Tell him you love him and demonstrate it at every opportunity.

Suppose you don't feel in love with your husband? As we

discussed earlier, act the way you want to feel. Your feelings will catch up with your actions.

### Cold, Indifferent Husbands

There are some men who have grown cold towards their wives and may shun them no matter what they do or what words they use. How can a woman show love to her husband in that case? By her behavior, empowered by the Holy Spirit. By patiently, steadfastly, demonstrating her love in every way. Jesus loved those who were cool to Him, even those who hated Him. He loves you and me, and we are not always lovable either. We also grow cool to Him at times, yet He continues to love us. Ask Him to work through you, to enable you to show love to a husband that has grown cold. Ask Him to love your husband through you.

### Reverence: To Enjoy

Enjoy: to rejoice over; to have a good time with; to take pleasure or satisfaction in.[10]

If you were asked to list several things in life that you enjoy, what would you place on that list? An unexpected note from a friend? A warm, spring day? A relaxing evening spent with those closest to you?

Would your husband's name appear on the list?

### Ideas

A simple way to enjoy your husband is to do special things for him. Ray is a man who treasures the simple things in life and appreciates every effort I make to please him, even if he doesn't always say so. So for him, some special things might include:

- Coffee in bed
- Setting aside time to trim his hair (I learned to do this practicing on our sons when they didn't know how hair was supposed to look!)
- A seafood dinner, preferably fried, or banana pudding like his mom used to make
- Watching the Nebraska Cornhuskers play football (especially if they are winning)
- A surprise gift from his favorite store
- Exclaiming over his freshly mowed lawn as I bring him ice water and a cool, wet towel
- Planning a trip to see our children
- Catching a matinee at the movies

Consider giving your husband small presents or surprises. We know of one husband who suddenly discovered hair growing on his ears, as it has a tendency to do as men age. His wife found a personal grooming kit for men at a local department store. It was small and inexpensive and had special scissors that were made for clipping those wandering hairs. She purchased the kit and put it in her husband's drawer. No words were ever spoken, but she could sense his appreciation and love when he discovered it.

It doesn't take a lot of time, effort, or money to let your husband know that you enjoy him and want to do things for him. If your husband likes a certain kind of cookie, slip a bag into his suitcase on his next trip. Discover what his interests are and become involved.

If there's something he *dislikes,* don't insist that he do it.

I (Connie) love to go for drives. My family did this when I was growing up, and it was a special time for all of us. However, my husband considers them a waste of time. Early in our marriage, I was determined that he would enjoy these drives as much as I did. "Just give them a chance," I would say in exasperation.

"Drives are not relaxing to me," he'd reply. "Drop me off at home first, and then go on your drive."

*Where's his sense of fun?* I'd think. Finally, it dawned on me that it was okay if he didn't want to go. What if he insisted I do something I disliked? I wouldn't appreciate that, yet that was exactly what I was doing to him. I quit lecturing and cajoling and started taking drives when he was working or tied up with something else.

### The Time Is Now!

Do you find that there's just not time to enjoy your husband? Try to creatively figure out a way to build this into your schedule. Life is too short to wait. Take a lesson from a good friend of ours whose husband died while still in his forties. Although they had twenty wonderful years together, she says, "I wish I had enjoyed him more when he was living. Life was usually so busy and frantic that we didn't take time for each other, especially after the kids came. We put our relationship on hold, thinking that one day the kids would be gone and then there would be time for each other again. We were wrong. He was gone before the kids were."

Think of a way to let your husband know that you enjoy him, and then do it. We believe it is something you will never regret.

### POSTSCRIPT

This chapter has been chock full of information, instruction, and ideas. Perhaps you are mulling over some of what you've learned, or maybe you have already begun to introduce some of these principles into your marriage.

In talking with dozens of women who are attempting to do what you have just read about, there is a question that comes up over and over again: When will my husband start doing *his* part?

Most women are willing to put these principles to work in their marriages, *up to a point*. And so they begin. The first few days fly by quickly. Because the wives are still excited and motivated, the next few weeks speed by as well. Before long, though, fatigue begins to set in. They may be expecting or hoping that their husbands will notice their efforts, and that may not be happening. Their resolve weakens, yet they continue on, often at a slower pace. Before long, their energies fail. The excitement ebbs. They begin to ask if it wouldn't be a good idea if someone taught their husbands what their responsibilities were. They are tired of, as they see it, doing all the work. They become worn out and discouraged.

"If only my husband would do just a portion of what I'm doing, I could keep going," said one woman, "but he's not doing a thing. And he's not even noticing my efforts. If he's not going to notice, I'm going to save myself the trouble. I am no longer going to do this."

And so she stopped. Don't let her story be yours as well. Don't stop! Don't "save yourself the trouble." What you are doing isn't trouble. What you are doing is God's will!

One young woman we know had begun incorporating many of these things into her marriage. It was exciting for the first three weeks, but then she began to have second thoughts. Her old way of life felt more comfortable and, as she told us, "I thought to myself, *Why should I do all of these things for him?*"

Just then her three-year-old daughter came into the room. She told her child, "It's time to brush your teeth."

To which her daughter replied, "Why should I?"

*Why should I?*

Mothers, could it be that one reason your children are not obeying you is that you are not obeying what your heavenly Father tells you to do? Are you reaping what you are sowing?

Don't let your motive for doing this be *only* because you want your husband to notice, or your marriage to change or life to get better. Do this also because it brings honor and glory to Jesus Christ. If your husband notices, great! If he doesn't, that's fine, too. You are not doing it because of *him*. You're doing it because of *Him*. The key is to stop focusing on yourself and your rights and start focusing on Jesus Christ and your role.

Honestly ask yourself why you are doing this:

For yourself?

>Your husband?

>>Your kids?

>>>*Or for the Lord?*

## HOW ABOUT YOU?

Are you willing to apply these principles but only up to a point? If so, at what point will you decide to go back to your old ways of disobedience to the Lord?

Don't be an "up to a point" kind of woman. Don't be just a starter—be a finisher! Don't quit the work God has called you to do.

The Bible tells us that after Peter denied Jesus for the third time, Jesus turned and looked into his eyes, and Peter went outside and wept bitterly. One day Jesus will look into your eyes. You will give an account to Him of how you have lived your life. What will you say in the area of being a godly wife? Will it be a joyful recollection, or will it be filled with bitterness and regret? Will it be joy? Or will it be despair? The choice is yours, and you can bring glory to God by the choice that you make.

## CHAPTER 6 SUMMARY

1. When we respond to God's directive to be pure, we activate a safeguard in our marriages.

2. Purity and reverence may be the instruments God uses to win a disobedient husband to His Word.

3. Reverence has many aspects. Nine were included in this chapter.

4. God desires our obedience, and implementing His principles in our marriages is pleasing to Him.

5. Don't follow these principles only "up to a point." Get rid of the "point." Wholeheartedly follow them out of your love and obedience to Jesus Christ.

Chapter 7: Holy Beauty

We live in a world today that puts tremendous emphasis on external appearances. People are flocking to gyms in droves, searching for better bodies. Imaginary stairs are climbed and bicycles going nowhere are madly pedaled. Women are sweating to the oldies and the not so oldies. Oh, surely if we work a little harder, we can be ten pounds thinner by summer. Cosmetic sales are soaring, and age-defying products are flying off of the shelves as never before in our quest to stay young. We have become a nation bent on maintaining youth and beauty at all costs. This is especially true if you are a woman.

There is an overabundance of material that tells us that if we are attractive outwardly, then we are more valuable, more desirable, more respectable, and surely rank higher in the pecking order of life. Recently, an ad in a women's magazine touted makeup as a woman's most important accessory for today's living.

We agree completely. A woman's makeup is not merely her most important accessory, but the most important thing about her, period. Her inner makeup, that is. We call this "holy beauty." It is not based on the world's standard of beauty. It is based on the Lord's standard. It is a beauty that God calls unfading. We are told how we can have it in His Word. It doesn't have to be wiped on, rubbed in, ripped off, or reapplied in the morning. It is a twenty-four-hour-a-day beauty package, and it can be yours, if you are willing to be obedient to God's Word.

*Holy beauty...God's idea of beautiful!*

# Holy Beauty

*She is forever beautiful,*
*the one who resembles Christ.*

She was barely five feet tall and had to stretch to see above the steering wheel when she drove. Her hair was a beautiful silver gray, her face caressed with wrinkles. Joy danced in her eyes, and she spoke with a lilt in her voice. She was so magnetic, yet her life seemed so ordinary. What made her the way she was? I (Connie) couldn't quite figure it out. I was a young girl, and she was my great-aunt.

When I was nine years old, she gave me a Bible with my name inscribed on the front in gold lettering. Up to this time, I had shared one with my sisters. Now I had my very own. I was so proud! As she gave it to me, she said it was the greatest book I would ever possess. Just by the way she held it in her hands told me she dearly loved it.

Like my family, she lived on a farm, and it was only a few miles away from us. The country house had been made charming by her special touch. The single bathroom, with a claw-foot tub, was accessible only by first walking through two bedrooms. The kitchen was small, but oh, the generosity and love that was generated when a special treat or a meal was shared with a guest. Every time we visited, announced or unannounced, we received a grand welcome. "You've just made my day," she'd say cheerfully, "How kind of you to visit. Come in! Come in! Come in!"

She had known hard times and heartache, but she bore no ill will or bitterness. These were foreign words to her. She loved to attend church, but her husband was not a churchgoing man. Never do I recall her complaining or wishing aloud to my mother (when we girls were listening from an adjoining room) that he would go with her. "He's in God's hands," she'd say. She loved him with a loyalty and fervor that was rare even then. She treated him as a prized jewel, although he wasn't one to display such emotion in return. She neither gossiped or judged, and she had a way about her that made you want to behave in the same manner.

I observed all of this for some time, and, even as a young girl, I knew she was special. Although she lived an everyday kind of life—her world humble, her days predictable—she radiated something that made me want what she had.

It would be years before I realized what it was that made her so special. She had committed her life to Jesus and lived it trying to be like Him. Because of that, she had been transformed from the inside out. *She was holy beautiful.* What I had observed for years was a reflection of what He had done in her life. She had a beauty that came straight from the Maker Himself. No wonder I was so attracted to her.

Holy beauty, unlike external beauty, never fades, and in fact, is enhanced with each passing year. It's the ultimate beauty product, and it is produced in us by God Himself. That's what we'll be discussing in this chapter, but first we'll look briefly at external beauty.

## EXTERNAL BEAUTY

Say what you will, a woman's external appearance *is* important to her husband. As a friend of ours says, "If you ask one hundred men if their wife's appearance matters to them, ninety-five of them will say yes, and the other five won't have understood the question!"

When I (Nancy) was a little girl, my mother would actually change her clothes and mine before Dad came home. Somehow, that heightened the anticipation of his arrival. She wanted us to look nice when he came home from his workday, and he always seemed to appreciate that she did this.

In many households today, both the husband and wife work outside of the home. We believe that all women are working women—either in the home, out of the home, or both. Every woman's role is vital and touches dozens of lives around her. How much time you have to freshen up at the end of the day depends on your personal circumstances. Some women have ample opportunity to do this, while some don't. Regardless, it is a fortunate man who has a wife who makes an effort to look nice for him.

## A Man's Perspective

It's a well-known fact that men are more visual than women. It is one of the ways we're different. If you show a man a picture of an attractive woman, frequently his eyes will linger on it. If you do this to a woman, showing her a picture of a nice-looking man, often his appearance won't even register in her mind.

I (Connie) remember many years ago visiting a newlywed couple who were friends of ours. We decided to drive to the ice cream shop for dessert. The wife ordered two scoops of vanilla. Her husband suggested she get just one. She assured him she wanted two. He assured her he thought one was more than enough. After energetically discussing the issue for a few moments, she turned and left the store without buying anything.

*Most men wish that they were able to see beyond the external to the internal, but few are able to do so.*

We saw these friends recently and laughed at the memory. Our friend readily admitted that what he was attempting to do was make certain that his wife's physical appearance stayed the same following the wedding. "I hope I no longer try to control her like that," he said, "but I can't say enough about how much I appreciate her staying in shape after all these years. I think if any man was honest, he'd have to say that his wife's physical appearance matters greatly to him."

It's frustrating to many women that men place such a high value on external appearances. To a woman, this seems superficial and relatively unimportant. It's difficult for her to understand why this often seems to carry as much or more weight with her husband as her inner beauty.

We talked to several men to glean insight into this matter. Their opinions, though varied in degree, all came down to the same basic conclusion that most men wish that they *were* able to see beyond the external to the internal, but very few are able to do so. As one man said, "I don't know why men are so visually stimulated. I'd like to say I'm not, but I am! I know this sounds awfully shallow, but that's the way it is. I'm in a large Bible study, and it's an issue for every man in the group. We've talked about it many times. Men are visual creatures. It is an ongoing struggle and temptation is never far away, even for godly men. Not the temptation to fall into adultery, perhaps, but certainly the temptation to look too long or imagine too much. You can hardly go to your mailbox anymore without this issue hitting you in the face."

Continuing, he said, "It makes a world of difference to a man when his wife *makes an effort* to look nice for him. To a man, this shows love, care, and respect for him. Men see their wives as a reflection of themselves. Frequently, we are around well-dressed women all day long in the workplace. To come home to a woman who is disheveled and unkempt is not something to which any man I know looks forward. I think if wives realized how important this is to their husbands, they might more easily consider changing."

This can be a difficult issue for a man to broach with his wife. Said one man, "I don't mention this issue anymore, because my wife becomes extremely defensive and argumentative. She accuses me of not loving the 'real' her. In an effort to keep the peace, I no longer bring it up. However, my desire for her to look nice hasn't changed. The only thing that has changed is that it's no longer verbalized. It's still an issue to me, just an unspoken one."

Most men care how their wives look, whether they verbalize it or not. A wise woman would consider giving some thought to this and asking God if this is an area that needs some work. Without making any announcements, you might begin to make needed improvements. Do it with a joyful, glad heart, and don't get discouraged if he doesn't say anything. Many times it is awkward for a husband to say much, especially if there's been conflict in the past. Not only will you enjoy doing this for your husband, but many women find this makes them feel better about themselves as well.

### Exercise

Is exercise a part of your schedule? Women are busier than ever before, yet often exercise actually gives them a renewed sense of energy. Most experts recommend exercising at least three times a week for twenty to thirty minutes or more each time. It is good for you not only physically, but emotionally as well.

Some women get up early to fit exercise into their schedules. Many have found that it helps to exercise with a partner or in a group. This provides companionship as well as accountability. One woman we know walks every morning and uses this time to pray and reflect on the Lord. Is exercise a must for the godly woman? No! Some women are physically unable to do so. But for those of you who are able, you might find it beneficial.

### Other Ideas

The ways for a woman to care for her external appearance are innumerable. Magazines are replete with simple tips. Fix your hair in a flattering way. If you don't have much time, find a low maintenance cut that works well for you. You can wear inexpensive jewelry to offset your clothes, or, if you're so gifted, you might find a scarf that makes an outfit really shine. There is a huge assortment of women's clothes to choose from these days, which fit all sizes and budgets. We both frequent consignment shops and find things that work for us at a fraction of their retail prices. A minimal amount of makeup can go far in making you look your best and takes just moments to apply.

Have you noticed that when you wear an old shirt with paint stains, and your husband's oversized sweat pants, you actually feel tired? Try taking the time to dress for your day, and don't sacrifice looking nice for comfort. It is easy to have both. Most women wear 20 percent of their clothing 80 percent of the time. Find clothes that work for you and that you can see yourself wearing immediately. If you catch yourself thinking, "I'll probably wear this sometime" when you're considering purchasing an item, chances are you won't! Put it back on the rack and find something that you'll wear often. It doesn't take long to distinguish between what you will wear often and what you'll hardly wear.

### A Surprise Party

I'll (Nancy) never forget attending a "come as you are" birthday party. The ones who planned the event had selected several drivers to pick up the invited women around nine-thirty at night.

I was quite surprised when our doorbell rang. We had just put our four young children to bed. When I answered the door, I had only enough time to grab my purse before being whisked away to the hostess's home.

There were about twenty of us who had been invited, and we

knew one another well. What fun it was for us to suddenly find ourselves out for an impromptu evening. As we talked about our rapid getaways, we began to look at each other. Normally at such a gathering, we all looked our best. But not that night! Most of us were embarrassed. Traces of lipstick gave evidence of faces that had been fussed over much earlier. Almost everyone's hair had not seen a brush in hours. And where in the world did we get those old sweat pants, unmatched tops, and ragged bathrobes? After perusing one another's outfits, our eyes rested on one friend in particular, and the questions began:

"You knew about this, didn't you?" we said in chorus.

"No!" she exclaimed. "Why would you think that?"

"Because you look so nice," we told her. "Your hair is in place, you're wearing a matching outfit, and you have on fresh lipstick. You look better than we do when we're getting ready to leave the house!"

"Really, I didn't know," she exclaimed, but we were not convinced. Obviously, she took far more care with her dress at home than the rest of us did. *Blessed is the husband whose wife pays attention to the way she looks for his sake, as well as her own.*

The woman commended in Proverbs 31 wore good clothes—fine linen and purple (Proverbs 31:22, NASB). However, this is not to be the focal point of who you are. More important than this by far, is the hidden person of your heart.

## INNER BEAUTY

Let it be the inward adorning and beauty of the hidden person of the heart, with the incorruptible and unfading charm of a gentle and peaceful spirit, which (is not anxious

or wrought up, but) is very precious in the sight of God.
(1 Peter 3:4, AMP)

What makes a woman beautiful? It is the imperishable quality of a gentle and quiet spirit. There will come a time in your life when your physical beauty will fade. There will also come a time when your sexuality is not as enticing to your husband as it is now. What are you doing presently to prepare for these future changes? Are you allowing God to develop your *inner beauty?*

How can you develop the qualities of a gentle and quiet spirit? You *cultivate* them.

## A Gentle Spirit

What does it mean to be gentle? One of the definitions may surprise you:

Gentle: to belong to a family of high station, of noble birth.[1]

It is incredible to realize that a Christian *is* of noble birth, born into the family of God.

To be gentle is to be free of harshness, sternness, and violence. Do you scream at your children or husband? Do you have a quick temper? Try softening your voice—it's surprising to see a child respond to the whispers of his mother and a husband blossom because of a soft-spoken wife.

Choose to be a gentlewoman! Our definition of a gentlewoman is: one who is born again, submissive to, and surrendered to the lordship of Christ.

Jesus was gentle and humble in heart (Matthew 11:28–30,

NASB). Don't you want to become like Him? The more you learn about Jesus and surrender to Him, the more this will happen. Quite simply, if you want to be like Jesus, you must learn of Him.

## A Quiet Spirit

Peacefulness is becoming a valuable commodity in our culture. Have you noticed that it is for sale these days? Aroma therapy, candles, soaps, creams, and elixirs all claim to be the antidote for stress in a complicated world. Small, soft lavender-scented pillows or bedside machines that mimic the sound of waves, rain, birds, and wind are helping the sleeping habits of the restless.

But what can compare to a *spirit* that is *peaceful*—not anxious or overwrought? No price tag can be put on a soul that is tranquil, calm, and still—free from noise or uproar. That comes from having a right relationship with God and is freely offered by Him.

> Peace I leave with you. My peace I give to you; not as the world gives do I give to you. Do not let your heart be troubled, nor let it be fearful. (John 14:27, NASB)

### Practical Tips

Here are some simple, practical things a woman can do to maintain a quiet spirit.

- Start the day with prayer.
- Spend time with and abide in Christ.
- Ask for God's help in developing a quiet spirit.
- Grocery shop for a week with a complete list.
- Don't go to bed, if possible, with the kitchen and living areas

unsightly. (This causes you to begin the next day behind schedule.)

- Watch your caffeine and sugar intake.
- Don't overcommit yourself.
- Don't sign your children up for excessive time in after-school sports and lessons.
- Plan for a day at home—we call them "home days"—and put them on the calendar.
- Don't overspend.
- Try to fold the laundry as it comes out of the dryer. We timed ourselves on this. The first load took two minutes. The second load took two minutes and ten seconds. If you let the clean laundry pile up, it may take you several days to get it put away because it becomes so overwhelming.
- Take a bubble bath. You can purchase a small tub pillow to lean against; read an uplifting book as you soak.
- Put the children to bed earlier.
- Play praise music.
- Ask your husband to massage your shoulders and neck; offer to do this for him if he enjoys it.
- Forgive quickly; don't bear grudges.

### Hope

> For in this way in former times the holy women also, who hoped in God, used to adorn themselves, being submissive to their own husbands. (1 Peter 3:5, NASB)

Your hope in God is a necessary part of developing inner beauty. To be holy beautiful, you must believe in God and also *hope* in Him.

Hope is to:

cherish a desire with anticipation and to expect with confidence and trust that God is working on your behalf.[2]

Sarah placed her hope in God. How wise she was, and what a
leap of faith her life demonstrates to us. For ninety years she had
been childless, and she had come to deeply regret her own plan
that Abraham should have a child with her maid, Hagar (Genesis
16:1–16). Then one day the Lord appeared to Abraham and told him
that the next year Sarah herself would have a son. Sarah laughed
when she heard this, saying, "After I have become old, shall I have
pleasure, my lord being old also? After the Lord Himself confronted
her revealing to her that He knew her thoughts, Sarah's faith was
born (Genesis 18:1–15). She placed her hope and faith in God and
considered Him faithful who had promised. And what God had
promised came to be just as He said it would. Sarah gave birth to
Isaac.

Sarah is given to us as an example of a woman who obeyed her
husband and responded to him as the leader of her household. And
God considers this so noteworthy that He puts her in His "Hall of
Fame" as one who triumphed in her faith (Hebrews 11).

Where do you place your hope? Sarah placed hers in God,
expectantly and with confidence. She knew God would do as He
said even though she had never conceived a child as a young
woman. It would seem she anticipated that God would work on
her behalf even in the most difficult circumstances.

## The Key

Peter, who gives us Sarah as an example, tells us:

You are now her true daughters if you do right and let nothing terrify you [not giving way to hysterical fears or letting anxieties unnerve you.] (1 Peter 3:6, AMP)

Fearlessness seems to be intertwined with a woman's choice to acknowledge her husband's leadership. If you are a fearful person, ask yourself: "Have I taken the leadership of the home away from my husband and neglected verbal and heartfelt acknowledgment that my husband is responsible *before God* to be the leader?"

To take over the leadership in the home, it seems to us, results in emotional unrest and fearfulness in the heart of a wife.

## Are You a Controlling Woman?

In a recent discussion, a woman confessed to being a "control freak." As she described herself and her controlling ways, she acknowledged that she had indeed become a very anxious woman. Examine yourself if you are fearful. Could it be that you need to give back the leadership role in your family to your husband?

To do this involves a conscious decision on your part. Once you do this, don't be quick with "constructive" criticism or second-guess your husband. If you've led the family for any length of time, give him a while to hit his stride. Encourage him! Both of you will be blessed by God as you fulfill your roles. Remember, your hope is in *God*, not in your husband and his abilities.

## Consideration

> In the same way you married men should live considerately
> [with your wives], with an intelligent recognition [of the
> marriage relation] honoring the woman as [physically] the
> weaker, but [realizing that you] are joint heirs of the grace
> (God's unmerited favor) of life, in order that your prayers
> may not be hindered *and* cut off [Otherwise you cannot pray
> effectively.] (1 Peter 3:7, AMP)

Your husband should live as considerately with you as you do with
him. He should honor and respect you as a joint heir of grace. That
is what God expects him to do, and the Bible says that his prayers
will be hindered if he doesn't. When your husband fails to treat you
with respect, his prayers are ineffective. *It seems to us that a woman
can help her husband in this regard.* How can she do this?

She can choose behavior that her husband can respect. She can
be cooperative and pleasant. A friend recently said to us, "I don't
know if my wife knows how much I love her, but I know for certain how much she loves me because of the way she treats me and
how she behaves towards me." This same man, at a Valentine's ban-
quet, was asked to list ten things he valued in his wife. His number
one reason: "I love the way she loves me." What a fortunate man!
And what a godly woman! Surely that's the way God intended it to
be. Even if a wife fails to do this, it is still the husband's responsibility to love his wife. There will come a day when he will answer
to God regarding this issue.

Can you imagine what your home life would become if both of
you respected, loved, and supported each other—even if one of
you is having a bad day?

### The Road That Matters

Regardless of where your marriage is at this point, you are in the place of blessing when you choose to do what is right. One aspect of doing so is striving to have a harmonious home. Peter sums up what he has been saying when he states:

> Finally, all of you, live in harmony with one another; be sympathetic, love as brothers, be compassionate and humble. (1 Peter 3:8, NIV)

These virtues are Jesus' own character. He lives in you and can exhibit these traits through you.

### Loving the Unlovable

Isn't it simple to live in harmony when your husband is treating you well? But what if he's not? How do you treat your husband when he is being unloving and moody? Listen to what Jesus says in regard to difficult relationships:

> Love your enemies. Let them bring out the best in you, not the worst. When someone gives you a hard time, respond with the energies of prayers for that person. If someone takes unfair advantage of you, use the occasion to practice the servant life. No more tit-for-tat stuff. Live generously.
>
> Here is a simple rule of thumb for your behavior: Ask yourself what you want people to do for you; then grab the initiative and do it for *them!* If you only love the lovable, do you expect a pat on the back? ...I tell you, love your enemies. Help and give without expecting a return. You'll

never—I promise—regret it. Live out this God-created identity the way our Father lives towards us, generously and graciously, even when we're at our worst. Our Father is kind; you be kind.

Don't pick on people, jump on their failures, criticize their faults—unless, of course, you want the same treatment. Don't condemn those who are down; that hardness can boomerang. Be easy on people; you'll find life a lot easier. Give away your life; you'll find life given back, but not merely given back—given back with bonus and blessing. Giving, not getting, is the way. Generosity begets generosity. (Luke 6:27–37, *The Message*)

One way you can tell that you are walking in the Spirit in your marriage is to ask: Is my husband's response my goal, or am I doing this to please the Lord?

God will enable you to be compassionate to someone who doesn't deserve it, just as He was and is to you.

Ask yourself, "Why is my husband moody and sharp with me?" Often the answer is that you are simply catching the overflow of what happened to him at work, with his parents, or with some other problem. *Is this fair?* No, but life isn't always fair. Consider other reasons as well: Is he stressed about something in particular? Is he fatigued due to extra hours he's putting in at work? Is he going through a difficult time with someone? Ask God to give you understanding and patience during these times and continue to treat your husband lovingly, regardless of how he may be treating you.

Don't be so sensitive personally that you let your feelings and emotions be set by another's treatment of you. Jesus didn't do that.

He continued to live His life with honor, dignity, love, and mercy through the most difficult times. Don't be judgmental or unfriendly. Don't allow yourself to be too easily wounded, crushed, or hurt. Guard against bitterness by being quick to forgive. Ask Jesus to help develop these attitudes in you when you face challenging times.

### Be a Blessing

Your job is to bless and be a blessing (1 Peter 3:9, *The Message*). Put another way, it reads like this:

> Never return evil for evil or insult for insult (scolding, tongue-lashing, berating) but on the contrary blessing [praying for their welfare, happiness, and protection, and truly pitying and loving them]. For *know that* to this you have been called, that you may yourselves inherit a blessing [from God]—that you may obtain a blessing as heirs, bringing welfare and happiness and protection. (1 Peter 3:9, AMP)

Holy, beautiful women never return harsh words, but instead give a blessing back! One way to do this is through prayer. Do you see that the blessed outcome of our unselfish prayer for the welfare, happiness, and protection of our husband is that we may inherit these things as well?

Have you and your husband ever been in the following cycle? He raises his voice; you raise yours. He becomes louder; you retaliate.

This pattern is an endless cycle, but the dynamics of it are broken quickly if you no longer react. You can *choose* to no longer react, but act instead in a manner the Bible says is right. In this case, your consistent, sweet, silent response to poor behavior may be the very thing God will use to change you husband. Don't give in to the urge to let your silence be cold and stony.

When Jesus was oppressed and afflicted, He did not open His mouth (Isaiah 53:7; Matthew 26:63, 27:12–14, NASB). Mark says that Pilate was amazed at how Jesus stayed silent in the midst of the accusations that were swirling around Him. Only when He was placed under oath and asked whether He was the King of the Jews did He humbly reply, "Yes, it is as you say" (Mark 15:2, NIV).

If your husband is short-tempered and impatient, try remaining silent, in love. Stop participating in the vicious cycle of "he gets angry; I get angry." Choose not to react during heated times. Wait until your husband has had a chance to cool down or is more rested before discussing things.

*You can choose to no longer react, but to act instead in a manner the Bible says is right.*

Suppose you had two dogs. Let's say one was red, and the other blue. What would happen if you fed only the red dog and not the blue one? The red dog would become bigger and stronger, while the blue one became weaker. Over time, Red would thrive, while Blue shriveled away.

Every time you act in a loving way towards your husband, it's as if you're feeding the red dog and refusing to feed the blue one. *The basic principle is simple: Feed Red, and starve Blue!* Each time you do this, it becomes more and more a part of your natural response.

What you're doing is training your mind to think in a new way, and each successive time becomes easier.

Begin now to pray that you will have the strength to do this, and begin praying scripturally and fervently for your husband.

### How to Pray Scripturally

There is an example given in Colossians of a powerful way to pray. You might consider praying for your husband in such a way. Pray that he will:

- be filled with the knowledge of God's will,
- have spiritual wisdom and understanding,
- walk in a manner worthy of the Lord, living a life full of integrity,
- please the Lord in all respects, and do those things that bring glory to God,
- bear fruit in every good work,
- increase in the knowledge of God,
- be strengthened with all power according to the Lord's glorious might,
- attain steadfastness and patience,
- joyously give thanks to the Father, who has qualified us to share in the inheritance of the saints in the kingdom of light. (Colossians 1:9–12)

### *Pursuing Peaceful Relationships*

For let (her) who wants to enjoy life and see good days good—whether apparent or not, keep (her) tongue free from evil and (her) lips from guile (treachery, deceit)...Let (her) search for peace (harmony, undisturbedness from fears, agitating passions, moral conflicts) and seek it eagerly. Do not merely desire peaceful relations (with God, with your fellowmen, and with yourself), BUT PURSUE, GO AFTER THEM! (1 Peter 3:10–11, AMP, emphasis added)

We are to actively pursue peaceful relations, not just desire them or wait on them to come our way. Many times our hurt or pride paralyzes us and prevents us from seeking peace with our husbands.

Not long after I (Nancy) had begun to study and apply God's Word to my marriage, I was given an opportunity to live what I was learning. Our daughter Anne had been looking for a vintage 1966 Mustang automobile. She and her dad eventually found the perfect car: yellow with a black leather interior. Ray generously bought it for her and instructed her to watch the oil gauge since it was an older car and used oil more quickly. One day he got a call from Anne, who had just arrived at work.

"Dad, the car is acting strangely. I don't think it has any oil."

Ray was not pleased! We went to Anne's rescue, taking along our other daughter, Christine. As we drove, he verbalized his annoyance with Anne. Since I was completely innocent, I was quite unhappy to be hearing what he really should have been telling her.

We arrived at her workplace, and Ray replenished the oil. As we were driving home, he continued to express his disbelief that this could have happened after all the warnings he had given to her. I had not wanted to hear about it on the way over, and certainly I didn't want to hear about it all over again on the drive back! Yet what I had learned about pursuing peaceful relations with one's husband was fresh on my mind. With great effort, I chose to remain quiet.

This was new to me! My old reaction would have been to utter a few choice words. Instead, I thought about what had just happened. My husband is a wonderful man. He had graciously bought our daughter a beautiful car, and she had been careless with it. And instead of leaving her in the middle of a parking lot trying to figure out what to do, he came to her rescue willingly.

As we drove home, in the midst of his reprise of disbelief, I commented to him, "What a loving dad you are to help Anne when she didn't really deserve it." This comment mysteriously and completely defused him. He immediately returned to his pleasant self.

When we got home, our daughter Christine whispered to me, "Mom, how did you do that?"

"It was God's grace," I told her, and she knew it was true because she knew how I usually reacted.

There is no limit to what can happen in a marriage when you begin to apply what you've learned. The blessings are showered down not only on yourself, but on those around you. One of the sweetest is knowing that God is attentive to your prayers.

> The eyes of the Lord are upon the righteous and His ears are attentive to their prayer. But the face of the Lord is against those who practice evil. (1 Peter 3:12, AMP)

It is almighty God Himself who will oppose, frustrate, and defeat the one who chooses ungodly ways.

Life is full of opportunities to live out what you profess to believe, and you are being watched not only by your children. God is observing you as well. As He focuses on you and your life, is He pleased? Are you honoring the Lord by the way you embrace your role as a wife?

## CLASSIC BEAUTY

It is a wonderful thing to realize that when we live His way and through His power, something literally happens to us *inwardly* and *outwardly:*

> Our faces shining with the brightness of his face. And so we are transfigured much like the Messiah, our lives gradually becoming brighter and more beautiful as God enters our lives and we become like Him." (2 Corinthians 3:18, *The Message)*

This is classic beauty in the timeless sense. No blushes, powders, creams, or lotions can give what is being talked about here. *It comes from God alone.* As we allow Him entry into our hearts, the royal paintbrush of His glory is stroked across our lives, and we find ourselves becoming more and more like Him. This is the only beauty that really matters.

Holy Beauty.

Simply put, her makeup doesn't make a woman beautiful— Her *Maker* does!

CHAPTER 7 SUMMARY

1.  A woman's external appearance is important to her husband, yet it is not to define who she is.

2.  Our inner beauty is precious in the sight of God.

3.  We develop the qualities of a gentle and quiet spirit by cultivating them.

4.  Our hope in God is a necessary thing to developing inner beauty.

5.  It seems to us, that to break the God-given pattern for marriage results in emotional unrest within a wife.

6.  You can help your husband treat you with consideration by choosing behavior that he can respect.

7.  Women who belong to God are called to have harmonious homes.

8. One way you can tell if you are walking in the Spirit in your marriage is to ask: Is my husband's response my goal, or am I doing this simply to please the Lord?

9. You are to bless and be a blessing in your marriage.

10. Women with inner beauty pray for their husbands regularly.

11. You will obtain a blessing from the Lord if you are a woman with inner beauty.

12. A woman's makeup doesn't make her truly beautiful—her Maker does.

# Part 4

# Family Relationships

**M**y mother had the nerve to put me third. I asked her one day why she did things this way. She said first came God, then Daddy, then me. And that was the way He meant it to be. "I am third," I thought. Not liking the news, I decided to discuss it with my friend Lou. "Third," gasped Lou, "what a horrible spot. I'm first in my home, and I like it a lot." "What about God and your daddy?" asked innocent me. "Well, I'm first—I'm not sure who's two and who's three. I don't know much about God, but I sure outrank Dad. All he seems to do is make Mama mad. So I'm her number one girl; that's what she calls me. I'd lots rather be one, than dumb number three." The years went by, and I nearly forgot the talk that we'd had in the school parking lot. Until thirty years later, when I saw Lou again—oh, how I'd missed my dear childhood friend. "Do you remember our talk," Lou said to me, "about how your mom made you be number three?" My memory was fuzzy, but the impression was there. Lou looked at me longingly, then said with despair, "I'd give anything now, to be number three. I've learned about life—that's the way it should be. My mother was wrong to put me number one. She just didn't know how it should have been done. Your foundation was sure; mine was shaky at best. I never quite know how I fit with the rest." Lou let out a sigh and then uttered these words, "What a privilege it was for you to be third."

I went back to my mother's lovely small home in the same little town, where she now lived alone. Daddy had died just three years ago. Oh, how we miss him, you'll never know. My mother looked up as I came through the door. I looked at her gently, then stared at the floor. "Mom," I began, a small tear being shed, then I told her about what Lou had just said. My mother smiled softly and then said to me, "It wasn't my nerve that made you number three. It was my love—can you now understand? I was just carrying out God's almighty plan." It was her love. Of course! Now I see! Her love for God, for Daddy, for ME!

# CHAPTER EIGHT

# Reclaiming Your Priorities

*It is a life-changing thing to allow His priorities to become yours.*

**Y**ears ago, in a city near my hometown, I (Connie) was sitting with my family in a store where milk was sold. The store was quite old and a landmark of sorts. In addition to selling milk, it had a delightful stainless steel soda fountain where you could order ice-cream cones, banana splits, sundaes, and other delights. The family budget was tight and allowed little room for extras, so ordering from the fountain was a special treat for all of us. We usually did this in the summers after swimming in a nearby lake.

Vinyl-covered booths lined one wall of the store to provide additional seating. By the door an antique scale stood where you could weigh yourself. It was massive in size and seemed to me better suited for weighing heavy animals. The dial indicating your weight was so large that everyone in the store could see from wherever they sat. My sisters and I couldn't wait to get on the scale and weigh, and my dad usually did as well. My mother, however, never shared our excitement. This was a mystery to me at the time, although now I fully understand her reticence!

## "WHOM DO YOU LOVE THE MOST?"

On this particular occasion, we had gotten our order and were seated at a booth. I suspect we had already weighed ourselves three or four times. I distinctly remember looking across the table into my father's clear blue eyes and asking him whether he loved my mother or my sisters and me the most. Without hesitating, he said he loved each of us with all of his heart, but then he went on to explain that my mother held a higher position than we did in his life. That, he believed, was the way God intended it to be. His first love was for God, then for my mother, then for us girls.

I turned to my mother and asked the same question. She replied as my father had. "I love you dearly," she said, "but Daddy comes ahead of you girls." Was I discouraged or hurt? Not at all. I remember smiling from ear to ear as I licked my butterscotch revel ice-cream cone; I loved their answers to my question. It felt great knowing that they held one another in such high esteem, and it gave me a tremendous sense of security knowing we children couldn't uproot or supplant their relationship.

My family was not the exception. Most of my friends' parents felt the same way. Children, though greatly loved, ranked below the parents' commitment to each other. That was just the way it was, and as far as any of us knew, the way it was supposed to be. How quickly things can change, though, from one generation to another.

## A GENERATION LATER

As we've talked to women about their relationships in their homes, one thing has stood out time and time again: most women feel that apart from their relationship with God, their relationship with their children is the most important. Many knew their husbands should outrank their children, but the majority said that when it came right down to it, that is not the way it plays out in their homes.

As a result, the structure and hierarchy of family life have been turned topsy-turvy as women cater to their children's needs. Homes have become child-centered, and dads are often on the periphery looking in.

Not surprisingly, husbands often feel shunted aside and out of the loop. The marriage relationship is placed on the back burner, while the parenting relationship becomes all-consuming. Many women, feeling that they are the more gifted in parenting, frequently take the lead and relegate their husbands to the role of assistant.

Proverbs 20:15 tells us that "lips that speak knowledge are a rare jewel." Rare, as well, is the woman who puts her husband first in the home.

## PRIORITIES ARE IMPORTANT

When God formed Eve from the rib of Adam, His plan for the family was set in place. He created Eve to be a helpmate to Adam and relieve his aloneness. After this occurred, children were born into the family.

A wife's role is not meant to be abandoned or amended once children come along. Certainly it is expanded, but her commitment to her husband and her respect for his place in the family are to remain unchanged. Even though she is now a mother, she should still see herself as a helper to her husband.

God says that a man is to leave his father and mother and cleave to his wife (Genesis 2:24). A woman should not leave her husband—even in a psychological sense—and cleave to her children, yet that is what is being done in many modern households. To do this injures yourself, your family, and your relationship with God.

Marriage is intended to be the highest form of love and communication that exists between two people. To replace this relationship with the one you have with your children is to alter God's plan for your life and can be a roadblock in your marriage.

### The Family Vacation

The family was excited. Summer vacation was upon them and they were ready to head out for the eight-hundred-mile trip to their favorite camp in Minnesota. As the last bag was thrown into the trunk of the car, chaos broke loose. All three children scurried to sit in the front seat beside the driver. After much arguing, Johnny, the oldest, declared that since his legs were the longest, he should be allowed to sit up front.

Everyone loaded into the car according to the son's directions. Dad asked Mom if she wouldn't rather sit up front with him, but she insisted that she didn't mind the backseat at all, especially since this would please Johnny. He had been dubbed a natural born leader by his parents early on, so the fact that his preferences prevailed was not unusual.

When Mom decided to spell Dad at the wheel, Dad told Johnny to move into the backseat. Johnny turned to his mother and begged her to let him stay put. The pitiful look on the boy's face was all Mom could see. As her firstborn, he had always held a special place in her heart, and it was difficult for her to deny his request.

Mom turned to Dad and said, "I sat in the backseat for three hundred miles; you can too." In disbelief, Dad said that he had done his share of backseat sitting when he was a boy and had no intentions of doing so as a forty-year-old man. His remarks were greeted by a deafening silence from Mom.

Dad once again told Johnny to get into the backseat. Mom, in a clipped tone, said that Johnny would not be comfortable in the backseat because his legs were so long. Dad reminded Mom that he was two inches taller than Johnny. Johnny and his brothers waited in anticipation, knowing what the outcome would be. Sure enough, a few minutes later Johnny was back up front and stayed there for the duration of the trip.

As Dad said later to a friend, "The real issue isn't who sits in the front seat. The real issue is that my wife consistently puts our children ahead of me, and in doing so, she negates any sense of authority I attempt to model within our home."

Such is the scene as it is played out in various ways across America today. Women have somehow convinced themselves that they are doing a noble thing by putting their children first. They seem to feel as though this makes them a better parent and will result in a happier, more secure child. We believe that they are wrong. While women's priorities may have changed over the years, God's have not.

A professor at a Christian college recently addressed this issue. He said he feels that many parents today actually worship their children by unwittingly allowing them to be the authority in the home. In many Christian homes, he said, life often revolves around what pleases the children instead of what pleases God. So intent are parents on bonding with their children that they allow their marital relationship to flounder, and often their relationship with God is neglected as well.

The media-driven age in which we live tells us over and over again that the most important thing you can do for your child is to give them a strong self-image. While a healthy self-image is beneficial and even desirable, there is something that is far more foundational. It is teaching our children to love God.

> Love the LORD your God with all your heart and with all your soul and with all your strength. These commandments that I give you today are to be upon your hearts. *Impress them on your children.* Talk about them when you sit at home and when you walk along the road, when you lie down and when you get up. Tie them as symbols on your hands and bind them on your foreheads. Write them on the doorframes of your houses and on your gates. (Deuteronomy 6:5–9, NIV, emphasis added)

We are to be teaching our children about God *all of the time!* This is the most important thing that we can do for them. If children are taught this, their self-esteem is well on its way to being anchored securely.

How are the relationships in your life aligned? Where does the one with your husband rank? Your children? If more emphasis is placed on the latter, then you have fallen into the trap of placing your children first. This seems like a sweet thing to do, yet to do so denies your husband his rightful place in your life.

If you were to ask your husband, "Do you feel like I place you ahead of our children?" what would he say? I (Connie) once asked my husband that question, and he looked at me in a rather dumbfounded way.

"Are you serious," he asked? "The answer seems so obvious, I'm surprised you would have to ask."

His answer didn't surprise me; I knew it was true. I had been raised by parents who had consistently put each other first, and I had loved the fact that they did. Yet somewhere along the road, I had failed to do this in my own marriage.

What makes a woman do this? Many times her husband is not meeting her needs like she feels he should, so she will turn to her children in hopes that they will. Frequently she has become disenchanted in the marriage and refocuses her hopes and dreams on the lives of her children. Some women were raised in dysfunctional homes and are determined that their children will not experience the same upbringing that they did. Whatever the reason, if you sense that your priorities are out of order in your home, with God's help, begin changing them now!

## MOTHERING YOUR HUSBAND

I (Connie) once asked my husband the following question: "If you could choose one behavior for me to stop, what would it be?" I had begun to change in my marriage, and I was in a data-gathering mode.

His answer was immediate and to the point, "I'd want you to stop mothering me." He didn't have to think about it for a second. My mothering skills not only encompassed our children, but him too. Women often wonder where the romance has gone in their marriage. Yet as my husband explained to me, it is hard for a man to feel romantic towards a woman who is constantly mothering him, however well-intentioned she might be.

What might mothering one's husband look like in a marriage? We asked this question to a large group of both women and men. Almost without fail, criticizing their husbands' driving was at the top or near the top of the list. It's as if this is in a woman's DNA. Men, however, aren't interested in our helpful hints about how they can get somewhere faster, more safely, more scenically, or with less wear on the brakes. One woman told us this issue had become so touchy in her marriage that often she and her husband wouldn't be speaking to one another when they arrived at their destination. "Letting go of that was one of the smartest things I ever did," she told us. "We have so much more fun when we're out together. I no longer nitpick, and he no longer gets upset."

Another way of mothering your husband might be telling him how to dress. If he's under- or overdressed for an occasion, lovingly suggest he consider something else, but don't insist on it. Allow him his own style—don't force your preferences in fashion on him.

Generally speaking, unless he asks your opinion, let him dress as he likes.

Don't chastise or cajole him about leaving his clothes lying around. Certainly this isn't to say that you can't respectfully ask him to put his clothes away, but avoid nagging him if he doesn't do so immediately.

Don't micromanage his diet, his exercise, or how he spends his free time. Also, don't take it upon yourself to change things in his life that only he can change—i.e., smoking, cursing, gambling, etc. Again, there is nothing wrong with discussing behavior that concerns you, but do so in a respectful manner with the realization that it's not up to you to change your husband. Many times it is a wife's gentle, loving ways that prompt change in her husband as much as anything else.

For many couples, money is an area where the wife is tempted to mother her husband. It is degrading and insulting to a man for his wife to "hover" over his spending habits. If there is a real problem in this area, seek godly counsel. However, if it is simply a difference of personal preferences, don't try to control or manipulate your husband into doing things your way.

Mothering your husband takes a multitude of forms, and we've mentioned only a few. You might be surprised to hear what your husband has to say about it, as I (Connie) was. Consider asking his opinion. If he's feeling overly mothered, ask for practical suggestions on ways you could change. If he does express himself, don't become defensive and fire back at him why you do the things you do.

As one woman said, "I thought I could only tend to my husband *or* my children. There wasn't time or energy to do both. It was obvious who needed me more, so I took care of my children and mentally placed my husband on autopilot. I figured that one day when the children were gone, I'd work him back into my life, so to speak. However, as I began to reprioritize my relationships, I discovered that he didn't need tending as a mother tends to a child. What he needed was a wife. *And my children needed a mother who put their father first.*

"As one of my daughters told me years later when she was struggling with this same issue in her life, 'Mom, the best thing you ever did for me was to honor Dad like you did. There are so many days I find myself deferring to the children and shortchanging my husband. When this happens I think of your example, and this helps me get back on track.' I hadn't always been a mother who did this, but thankfully, this is what my daughter remembers."

The effects of prioritizing relationships are far-reaching. Not only does it influence your relationship with God and your husband, but most likely it influences the kind of spouse your daughter will be and the kind of woman a son may choose to be his wife. This may not always be the case, but often it is. God has given us the privilege of modeling priorities that not only honor Him and our husbands, but also influence our children to honor God more fully in their own marriages.

## THREE YEARS OR THIRTY?

Not long ago we were at a local restaurant, when a family was seated nearby. The family included a three-year-old girl, her parents, and her grandparents. Even as they were seated, we noticed that the little girl seemed to call the shots. She insisted on being seated in a high chair even though the rest of the group preferred that she sit in a booster seat. She then demanded that her two stuffed animals, which she had brought with her, be allowed to sit in their own high chairs. Many people in the restaurant sat and watched as chairs were rearranged to make room for what had now become three high chairs and four adult chairs. The little girl was the queen bee, and she had two members in her adoring audience: her mother and grandmother. The men sat silently at the far end of the table, staring at the menus.

Every word the little girl spoke caused the women to beam, but it appeared that the men didn't share their enthusiasm. Rarely did they speak, except to give an occasional answer to a direct question.

About twenty minutes later, a couple who had been seated near this group got up to leave. They stopped at the three high chairs and said something to the little girl. Then they turned to the adults and said, "She certainly commands all of the attention, doesn't she?"

"That's been going on for three years now," the little girl's father agreed.

"Three years?" the grandfather suddenly piped up. "It's been going on for a lot longer than that. Try thirty years," he said, indicating that this very thing had happened with this child's mother, his daughter. This remark was followed by awkward laughter as the couple left, at which point the men went back to eating their dinner, and the women went back to watching the child, their suppers untouched.

## WHEN GOD'S DESIGN IS ALTERED

To rearrange God's design for the family affects not only this generation, but those to come. Proverbs 22:6 tells us to "train a child in

the way he should go, and when he is old he will not turn from it."
If you are putting your children ahead of their father, you are training them in error. Home is the school that matters most. What our
children learn at home is what they will take with them when they
one day marry and have families of their own. We often think of
"training" our children as a verbal thing. What do we tell them?
What can we say to make them understand a principle? However,
"training our children" has as much to do with our actions as it
does with our words. If we are telling them one thing, but living out
something else, they are receiving conflicting messages about God's
Word, our convictions, and what it is we are teaching them.

## THE EFFECTS ON CHILDREN

When a woman holds her children in higher regard than she does
her husband, she is giving them an exaggerated sense of their own
self-worth. They come to believe that they are more important than
Dad, and frequently see themselves as more important than others.

Remember Johnny, from earlier in the chapter, who rode in the
front seat all the way to Minnesota? After leaving Minnesota, the
family veered off course to visit Johnny's grandparents. The first
morning there, Johnny came downstairs for breakfast. Two of the
chairs at the table had comfortable pads, but the others did not.
Johnny's grandfather was sitting in one of the padded chairs, so
Johnny sat in the other. The rest of the family was still asleep. After
getting the food on the table, Johnny's grandmother went to sit
down and noticed that Johnny was sitting in her chair.

"Johnny," Grandmother said, "you are sitting in my chair.
Would you mind if I sat there?"

"I want to sit here, Grandma," Johnny said. "The others are hard."

Both grandparents' eyes widened. After a word from his grandfather, Johnny grudgingly moved.

The same thing occurred at his uncle's house. Johnny walked into the living room and settled comfortably into the rocking chair. "Johnny, that is the rocker Grandpa always sits in," Johnny's uncle said. Johnny retorted that he'd sat in the chair first, then stomped from the room, leaving his embarrassed parents to cover the awkward pause that ensued.

Johnny had not been taught to respect his elders or to defer to those in authority over him. He was acting in the only way he knew and in the manner that he regularly saw modeled in his home—that priority should be given to him. Whether or not Johnny is a natural born leader, as his parents think, remains to be seen. The issue isn't whether our children are natural born leaders, but whether our children love and obey God. God help the family, business, or country led by a self-centered, natural born leader!

*Placing your children first seems like such a sweet thing to do, yet to do this denies your husband his rightful place in your life.*

Certainly we are not saying that you shouldn't adore your children. We adore ours. But we are saying that it is because we love them so much that we teach them about God's hierarchy and where they fit. God's love for them is just as g̲ṟe̲a̲t̲ ̲a̲s̲ ̲i̲s̲ ̲ for anyone else, but His plan includes respecting their elders and submitting to those in authority over them.

When you place your children first, you are treating your husband's position with disrespect and apathy, and you may well be teaching your children to treat him in the same manner. One woman told us that this occurred in her house for a number of years. She couldn't figure out why her children didn't have more respect for their father, because he tried so hard to be a good father to them.

"When I looked hard at myself and my priorities, I realized that I was the problem. By continually allowing the children to have precedence over my husband, I believe I was actually saying to them that their father's place, his opinions and preferences, were secondary to their own. I gave him no credibility, so why should they? When I began treating him as the head of our home and backing my words up with my actions, our children began respecting him as well."

Most children feel that their fathers are supposed to be the heads of their homes, but few will grant them this position unless it is modeled by you first. When parents are living in harmony within the home, it gives children a sense of peace and security that nothing can replace.

## GROWN CHILDREN

Even after children are grown, women often continue placing them ahead of their husbands. Adult children, especially daughters, can be extremely nurturing and warm toward their mothers. Don't let this draw you away from your husband or tempt you into giving your child more regard than you do him. This is not to say that you shouldn't enjoy or receive the attention given you by your adult children. Certainly this is a wonderful thing. But it is a reminder not to let this alter your husband's position in your heart and home.

If a woman is unhappy in her marriage, she will often turn to a son or daughter to provide her with the companionship she is not receiving from her spouse. It is not unusual to see women grieving as their children leave for college or get married. Part of this grief is natural and comes from the closing of a chapter in the child's life. Many times, though, much of the grief comes because a woman made an unhealthy choice to have children fill the emotional needs that her husband was meant to fill.

## HOW OUR HUSBANDS FEEL

How does it make a man feel when his wife puts their children ahead of him? We asked that question to a group of men. Their most common answers are listed below.

### 1. Insignificant and disrespected
Most replied that they felt a deep lack of respect from not only their wives, but from their children as well. "Respect is important to a man, and he doesn't feel that when the children consistently come first," said one man.

### 2. Unloved
Most men, unlike most women, associate love with actions instead of feelings. When a woman places her children above her husband, her actions say to him that she loves the children more than she loves him. Though not as vocal

about it as women, men desire to be deeply loved by their wives. It is difficult for a man to see his wife cherish the children, but treat him in a cool or casual manner.

### 3. Lonely

One of man's greatest needs is companionship, and a man usually expects to find this in his relationship with his wife. "As my wife pours more and more of her life into being a mother, she pours less and less of it into being my wife," said one man. "The friend I once had in my wife is now a friend to our children, but a stranger to me." The lonelier a man becomes, the more vulnerable he is to outside temptation. Is your husband lonely because of the time you spend with your children? Are you in any way making him more vulnerable to the attentions of other women?

### 4. Unappreciated

Men appreciate being appreciated! Many men feel that their wives show greater appreciation to their children than they do to them. "If our daughter goes to a friend's for the night, my wife misses her terribly," said one husband. "When she comes home the next morning, my wife is ecstatic to see her and acts as if she's been gone forever. I can be gone for days on a business trip, and my wife acts like I never left, and sometimes she even seems to resent my return home." Does your husband know how important he is to you and how much you value him? Are you an appreciative wife?

### 5. Resentment and Anger

Though not a majority, some men stated that when their wives put their children first, they felt a sense of resentment and anger, most towards their children, others towards their wives. "My fifteen-year-old son walks through the door, and my wife immediately asks about his day or rubs his back if he's tired. She pampers him constantly. I find myself resenting him, even though I know it isn't his fault." Is your husband frustrated or even jealous of your relationship with your children? Could it be that he feels left out or overlooked?

## IDEAS TO CONSIDER

Maybe you're sensing that you need a major overhaul in this area, or perhaps just some fine tuning. Regardless, here are some ideas to consider:

**1. Think positive thoughts.**
For every positive thought you have of your children, think of two for your husband. Begin noticing the many things he does. Perhaps he sees to it that the house is locked up every night or helps you replace the light bulbs. Men enjoy praise!

**2. Give him the benefit of the doubt.**
Often this comes easily with our children, but is more difficult with our husbands. Grant him the same gracious generosity that you so easily give your children.

**3. Be spontaneous.**
Surprise him once a week with a random act of kindness. One woman recently discovered that her husband liked a slushy drink that a local convenience store sold. She began

buying them for him. "He loves it when I do this. It's such a simple thing to do, and it lets him know I'm thinking about him."

**4. Invest in his stock.**

Share with your children things you admire about their father. This lets them see how important your marriage is to you. Though it's been said dozens of times, the way mom sees dad is the greatest influencer of how the children see him. Do this with others as well. Many women excel at communicating their children's strengths, but not their husband's. One woman pointed out that often friends will talk about their children in glowing terms, but when they talk about their husbands, they tend to talk about their weaknesses and inabilities. If you do this, stop! Commit to sharing with others only those things that build your husband up. Words are infectious and should be chosen wisely.

**5. Make your bedroom a haven.**

Too often this is the catch-all room. Make an effort to keep it clean, organized, and inviting. One woman bought a small love seat and placed it in the master bedroom. This is where she and her husband spend a few moments together once they've gotten in the door at the end of the day. It shows their children that they value each other's company as well. Burn a fragrant candle so that the room smells inviting and warm.

**6. Cater to his quirks.**

Many times we think our children's quirks are cute, but we think our husband's are obnoxious. One woman discovered that her husband liked his sheets changed often, yet she preferred going longer between changings. "I fought this for years," she said, "I thought he was being too obsessive. One day my daughter asked why I ignored her father's request for clean sheets, but always changed hers whenever she asked. I was shocked. I didn't realize I did this. I suddenly saw that I was not only dismissing one of my husband's rare requests, I was also modeling wrong priorities for my daughter."

**7. Check your attitude.**

Said one women, "I was stunned one night when my husband told me that he wished I had the same attitude toward him that I had toward the kids. From his perspective, I bent over backwards for them. I ran all over town to find my daughter the right dress or my son the right tennis shoes. But he said that if he asked me to stop on the way home at the hardware store and pick up a gallon of paint that would be ready, I balked." Our attitudes speak volumes to our husbands.

**8. Pray for your husband.**

This tip could go into every chapter. There is nothing like prayer to soften your heart and sharpen your focus.

**9. Reintroduce pet names into your relationship.**

Refrain from calling him "Dad" or "Daddy." Choose instead to call him by a name that shows your love and high regard for him as a husband.

Your husband may or may not respond as you reprioritize your relationships. It really isn't an issue, though, if you are doing it to honor God. Certainly it's nice for them to notice, and even appreciate, your efforts but it isn't necessary. *God notices.*

## REFLECTIONS ON PROVERBS 31

There was a time in my life when I (Connie) struggled greatly with this problem. The heartbeat of my soul was my children, and most of my energy went toward them. My husband, aware of how I felt, said little. Whenever the topic was discussed, I strongly defended the position I had taken. What could he say? I countered everything he brought up with my intention to give our children the best foundation possible. How could he argue with that?

In the midst of this, I sat down one morning to spend some time with the Lord. My Bible fell open to Proverbs 31.

"Interesting," I thought to myself. "I'll read through these verses and then go on to something else."

I began at verse 10:

A wife of noble character who can find? She is worth far more than rubies.

I agreed totally. But verses 11 and 12 stopped me cold:

Her husband has full confidence in her and lacks nothing of value. She brings him good, not harm, all the days of her life.

My heart was stirred as I read those words, and I felt the Lord asking me, "Connie, does your husband have full confidence in you? Does he lack anything of value? Do you bring him good and not harm all the days of your life?"

I attempted to justify myself before Him, but of course, it didn't work. He knows the innermost parts of my heart, and certainly He knew the truth.

"No, Lord," I finally answered, "my husband doesn't have full confidence in me. Sure he has confidence that I won't leave him for another man, or treat our children badly, or do something that is totally off-the-wall. But he doesn't have full confidence in knowing that when I say he's the head of our home, I mean it. Or that I will defer to his leadership when we disagree on something. He doesn't have full confidence in knowing that he falls right under You on my priority list, for he's not an idiot, Lord. He wouldn't delude himself into thinking he ranked second to You. Or third. Or fourth. No, Lord, my husband doesn't have full confidence in me."

"Does your husband lack nothing of value?"

"No, Lord, I cannot say that he does. Yes, I keep his shirts clean and his underwear drawer full, and I even put gas in his car for him; but I know, Lord, that these aren't the kinds of things You're talking about. I know that the things spoken of here aren't things you hang on a hanger, place in a drawer, or purchase at the gas station. No, I think You're talking about things like his feeling loved no matter what kind of day I've had or what kind of mood I'm in. Things like knowing he has my unwavering loyalty and that I'll be by his side, no matter what life throws at him. He knows I'd be by his side, Lord, but he might wonder whether it was out of duty or devotion. If he lacked nothing of value, he'd never have to wonder about that for a second."

"Does he lack something of value, Lord? Yes, Lord, he does. He lacks knowing I'll forgive quickly. He lacks knowing I won't pick a fight the minute he walks through the door if I'm irritable or upset. He lacks knowing that I care deeply about him because I get too busy and distracted to do that sometimes. He lacks knowing that impatient words will be a rarity in our home. He lacks knowing that his wife is no longer a scorekeeper. He lacks knowing that she no longer monitors his responses. Does he lack any of these things, Lord? Yes, Lord, some days *he lacks them all.*"

"Do you brings him good, not harm, all the days of your life?" Jesus asked.

Once again, the Lord probed my heart: "Does it bring him harm when he feels alone? Or when he feels battered by the world, but can't talk to you because you're too busy...too tired...too distracted...too caught up in the children? Does it bring him harm when he sees you taking care of everyone else in your life, except him? Or when he's trying to pray, yet things aren't right between the two of you because of your stubbornness? Does it bring him harm when you constantly correct him over the most insignificant things? Or when you are a better mother to him than you are a wife?"

"Do I bring my husband good and not harm all the days of my life, Lord? No, I don't, Lord. *Not even close.*"

I was struck by the paradox that though I didn't do those things for my husband, I easily did them for my children.

My children have full confidence in me. They know I make mistakes or forget things from time to time, but by and large, they know they can count on me 100 percent.

My children lack nothing of value. As much as possible, I make sure of that. Though not overly indulged materially, their physical, emotional, and spiritual needs are of utmost importance to me, and

I gladly attempt to make sure they are met. Yet I don't consider my husband's needs with the same regard. Or with the same urgency. *Or with the same joy.*

I attempt to bring my children good, not evil, all the days of my life. This is as natural as breathing for me as a mother, but not nearly as natural as a wife. There is nothing I wouldn't do for my kids. Yet I don't always do these things as eagerly for my husband, things such as taking his suitcase downstairs and putting it away. *You see, I was the woman in the story at the beginning of the book.*

I asked the Lord and my husband for forgiveness. I purposed to remember that this passage of Scripture is about a *godly wife, not a godly mother.* And from that day forward, I committed to prioritizing my relationships in a God-honoring way.

## ONE FUTURE DAY

One day your children will look back over their lives and reflect upon the people and events that helped mold them into who they are and what they believe. What will they see when they look at you? Will they see a mother who knew God's order for her life? Will they see a woman who took pleasure in being a godly wife? Or will they see a woman who chaffed and resisted God's role for her in her marriage? Will you stand before them as a mother who taught them to respect their father, because you respected him yourself? Or will they see a woman who treated her children with more dignity and love than she did her husband?

It is life changing to allow His priorities to become your priorities. Will you do this? Will you line up your relationships His way? By doing so, you become more usable to Him, and the plain, earthenware jug of your life becomes a vessel of honor that brings glory to God.

May you become a priority specialist!

For your husband…

For your children…

For future generations to come…

But most of all: *For the Kingdom of God!*

## CHAPTER 8 SUMMARY

1. To change the role that God intended for your husband is to chip away at the very foundation of your home.

2. When a woman puts her children ahead of her husband, he may feel insignificant, disrespected, unloved, lonely, unappreciated, and resentful.

3. The way in which you are raising your children affects not only them, but generations to come.

4. We are responsible for raising our children in a way that is pleasing to God.

5. Placing children ahead of their fathers often gives children an exaggerated sense of their own self-worth.

6. Husbands don't want us to be their mothers, they want us to be their wives. Children need mothers who are committed to loving their fathers.

7. Don't show favoritism to a certain child.

8. You want to be used as a vessel of honor by God. If your priorities are wrong, He can still use you, but it won't be in that way.

# Part 5

# The Motivation

The natural resistance to truly give ourselves to the other is rooted in our stubborn fear that if we really give, with no manipulative purpose, we will be shortchanged. Our needs will not be met. At best we'll be disappointed; at worst we'll be destroyed.

But God is faithful. We are to trust His perfect love to cast out our fear, believing that as we give to our spouse in His name, He will supernaturally bless us with an awareness of His presence. And He will. But it may take time—perhaps even months—before we sense His work in us. The willingness to give unconditionally does not come by simply deciding to be selfless. The stain of self-centeredness requires many washings before it no longer controls our motivation. Many commitments to minister and much time spent with God will transpire before we know what it means to give. Our job is to learn faithfulness and to press on in obedience, not giving in to discouragement or weariness, believing that God will always honor the conscious and persevering motivation to serve Him. When a spouse becomes critical, drinks more heavily, or rejects efforts of ministry, we are to continue in our obedience, believing that our responsibility before God is to obey and to trust Him for the outcome."[1]

*Marriage...created to be a ministry. Is yours?*

# Marriage Is a Ministry

*It is an amazing thing to realize
that as a woman serves her husband,
Jesus Christ considers Himself the One served.*

It was 6:00 in the morning, and I (Connie) was nearing the end of my run on the treadmill. I go regularly to my husband's place of employment and work out in the exercise room. A young woman whom I had never seen before came into the room, acknowledged me, and began walking on the treadmill beside me. She briefly looked over some note cards and then tossed them to the floor.

"Are you studying for something?" I asked.

"Yes," she replied, "I have boards coming up soon, and I'm trying to prepare for them."

After talking with her for a few minutes, I discovered that she was a fifth-year surgical resident and was six months away from completing the program. Written boards would follow, and she was beginning to review for them. She already had a job lined up in a nearby city.

She went on to say that she had just turned forty and had been married for five years. I asked her whether she thought her marriage was easier or harder than most, given the fact that she had waited until she was thirty-five to marry.

"You'd think it would be easier," she said, "but I'm not so sure. Marriage is hard. *Hard!* Far harder than medical school and residency combined."

Her bold statement piqued my interest, and I loved that she was so open and honest. "A friend and I are writing a book on marriage," I said, "so I find your comments fascinating. What do you think makes it so hard?"

"Do I have to be more specific than to simply say everything?" She laughed before going on. "I guess I would say that the most difficult thing to me is how marriage seems to boil down to two people reacting to one another. We didn't react when we were dating, yet now these reactions seem to define our marriage.

"Well," she continued, "I guess we did react when we were dating, but the reactions were positive. We were drawn to one another through them. But after the wedding, the reactions took a turn. Suddenly, it's one negative reaction after another, and instead of being drawn together, we've drifted apart."

I asked for an example, to which she replied, "Say my husband hurts my feelings. I express that my feelings are hurt and attempt to tell him why. He becomes defensive and says I'm too sensitive. I question his ability to gauge my sensitivity level and suggest he look into a course on sensitivity training. He responds with a remark of his own. Before you know it, we're not speaking to one another, and neither of us can even remember the original problem."

"What gets you back on track?" I asked.

"Usually, after a day or two, both of us grow weary of this behavior, and we begin to slowly treat one another with civility again. However, I can't help but believe that every time we do this, we get further and further from the marriage we had both hoped for because now, even when things are good, they're not all that great." She sighed and shook her head.

Her honesty and vulnerability surprised me. Here was a woman who would seem to have the world at her feet. She was attractive, intelligent, and pleasant. Very soon a successful medical practice would be hers as well. Yet here she was, at six in the morning, talking with a stranger about the pitfalls of marriage.

I then asked a penetrating question that had served as one of the turning points in my own marriage: "What is your motive for being married?"

A puzzled look crossed her face. "Motive?" she echoed, "What a strange question." With a chuckle she said, "I think of *murder* and *motive* going together, not *marriage* and *motive*. Let's see, what is my motive? Surely if I can get through a surgical residency, I can come up with a plausible sounding motive for marriage—but I can't."

She thought for a few moments more, but remained stumped. She had no idea what her motive in marriage was. *Do you?*

## MOTIVES

For years we were like the woman in the story. We had no idea that God had something to say about motive in marriage. One of us did not know the Lord, and although the other did, there was complete ignorance in this regard. We wanted to be happy in our marriages and hoped our husbands were as well, but frequently this was not the case. Once we began learning our job descriptions as wives, we quickly discovered that unless a woman's motive for her marriage lines up with God's plan, fulfillment and satisfaction will elude her.

The apostle Paul, inspired by the Holy Spirit, told us what God said about motives when he wrote this:

> Whatever you do, work at it with all your heart, as working for the Lord, not for men, since you know that you will receive an inheritance from the Lord as a reward. It is the Lord Christ you are serving. (Colossians 3:23–24, NIV)

Do you see it? It is the *Lord Christ* you are serving. That's the motive for your marriage. As you serve your husband, you are actually serving *Him*. What an incredible opportunity!

Too often we think of marriage as a relationship between two people. More than that, though, it is about our relationship with the Lord. Perhaps this is news to you, as it was for us at one time. Is it good news or bad?

Satan attempts to make you focus on yourself and what you want, as he did with Eve in the Garden. Doing this causes you to forget the "as unto the Lord" part of your marriage.

This passage is the nuts and bolts not only of marriage, *but of life itself.* This verse illustrates a simple but powerful process, and when you choose to implement it in your marriage, you will never be the same.

## WORK AT IT WITH ALL YOUR HEART

Whatever you do, you are to work at it with all your heart:
Cleaning the house.
Wiping a nose.
Visiting a neighbor.
Carrying out job responsibilities.
Serving in church.
*Being a wife.*

When work is done without putting your heart into it, the outcome is compromised and the process is stagnating and unfulfilling.

When I (Connie) was a young girl, my parents went to town one morning to buy groceries. They told my sister and me to go out to the garden and pick the green beans while they were gone. It was summertime, and we wanted to watch a few programs on television that we didn't normally get to see. This sounded far more fun than working in the garden. After a brief consultation, we decided that we would blitz the rows of beans, picking just enough to appease our parents. We grabbed two small sacks and filled them. We set the beans on the back porch, headed to our black-and-white television set, and eagerly turned it on. Ah, the rewards of a hard morning's work!

A few hours later our parents came home and asked if we had done our chores.

"Yes," we replied, I suspect a bit anxiously. We mentally crossed our fingers and hoped that would be the end of it.

"Where are the beans you picked?" my mother said, "I think I'll snap some for supper."

"On the back porch," I answered, suddenly wishing I had done a better job.

We heard the back door open and exchanged nervous glances as our mother went out. We then heard Mom conferring with Dad. He called us to the back porch, and, hearts dropping, we went.

"I thought you said you picked the beans," he said to us.

"Well, we kind of did," we said, trying our best to sound convincing.

"'Kind of' isn't good enough," he said. "When you've been given a job to do, you do it the best way you know how. I don't want to hear any more about this 'kind of' stuff. Now, go get a couple of sacks and let's go pick the beans."

Is that how you're living—in a "kind of" fashion? Can you see that if that's what you're doing, you're serving the Lord in that same manner? Don't you want to be a woman who serves Him with excellence? One way you can do this is by ministering to your husband. When you do, your motive and God's Word are aligned, and that is where deep satisfaction and peace lie.

## "TELL ME MORE"

One morning while we were working, a friend called. She asked how the writing was going. We told her we were in the middle of this chapter.

"It's about the whole idea of marriage being a ministry," we told her.

"Fascinating concept," she said, enunciating the words as only someone from England can. "I like that thought, although frankly, I must say that I have no idea what you mean by ministry. You see, I was raised in a church that didn't speak about ministry, so I'm a bit confused by the whole thing. I'd love to know more, though."

"Ministry" simply means "to serve." When a pastor comes to minister to a church, he comes to serve the people and the needs in that church. Ultimately, though, he is serving God.

That is what is meant by ministry in your marriage. As a wife, you are to minister to, or serve, your husband. As you do so, Jesus considers Himself served.

Marriage as a ministry was a life-changing concept for us and totally revolutionized the way we interacted with and served our husbands. Jesus Christ was now a part of the picture. Certainly we already knew He was in our midst, but when we realized that the way we treated our husbands was considered by Jesus to be the way we treated Him, it forced us to take a hard look at our actions in our marriages.

## BEGINNING TO CHANGE

Once you understand this concept, you can begin to see how the idea of ministry in marriage might bring changes to your life.

Let's say your husband has told you he'll be home at five-thirty in the evening and will be ready for dinner at six. Uncharacteristically, he's not home, and it's now six o'clock. The meal is ready, and the children (and you!) are growing hungrier by the minute.

Six-thirty comes and goes and still no husband. You decide to go ahead and feed the children and are cleaning up after them at seven o'clock, when your husband comes through the door. Normally, your first reaction might be, "Where were you? Why didn't you call? You're an hour late and dinner is cold." You want to let him know the inconvenience and irritation he's caused you.

However, if you view marriage as a ministry, your first thought would be for him. You would cheerfully greet him and ask if everything was okay. You would tell him how glad you are that he's home and graciously reheat his dinner. You might offer him compassion and warmth, letting him know how sorry you are that his day was so long. Certainly it's fine to ask him later on to please call the next time he's running late, but guard against doing so in an exasperated, judgmental fashion.

*More often than not, pride is what chokes out a ministering spirit in a marriage.*

Are you beginning to get the picture? Or does it seem rather one-sided to you? Could pride be rearing its ugly head? More often than not, pride is what chokes out a ministering spirit in a marriage. Did you know that God actually *resists* the proud? Proverbs 3:34 says that God resists the proud but gives grace to the humble.

There have been many times when I (Connie) have wrestled with pride in my marriage. When this occurs, ministering to my husband is the last thing I feel like doing. I know what I'm called to do—but I don't want to do it.

Why would God bless an attitude like that? Be assured, He doesn't! No wonder I feel so miserable when those times occur. I'm not only missing out on God's blessing, I am experiencing His *resistance* as well.

As you begin to minister to your husband "as unto the Lord," you may need to remind yourself, especially at first, why you are choosing to do this: You're actually serving Jesus when you serve your husband.

Our model is Christ Himself:

> But whosoever will be great among you, let him be your minister; And whosoever will be chief among you, let him be your servant: Even as the Son of Man came not to be ministered unto, but to minister, and to give His life a ransom for many. (Matthew 21:26–28, KJV)

Isn't it tempting to think about only wanting to be ministered to? Yet Jesus set the example for ministry: It is to be *others focused*. Once again you might be tempted to think that your ministry to your husband depends on him doing his part. So many times women tell us that things like this will work only if he does his part and that it has to be a mutual thing. But this simply isn't true. Your husband may *never* do his part. Does that give you permission to disobey Jesus' command? Of course not! Why would you allow someone else's ungodly choice to impact your own? How many times have you told your children to do what they know to be right, even if they're the only ones doing it? The same is true for you!

As you live this way, you will see seemingly small, trivial things in your life begin to change. Ministering will create great inroads to joy and peace into your marriage. I (Nancy) remember how this occurred in my marriage. This took place almost twenty years ago, yet it still comes vividly to mind.

## WHO WILL WALK THE DOG?

I had been a Christian for a short time when I heard a speaker who encouraged us to have a prayer time every morning. She suggested that we pray for one hour. I thought to myself *An hour? How can a person pray that long?* But I wanted to try.

About the same time, a friend asked me, "What does your husband do for you?" I thought. And thought. And thought some more. Never mind that I was able to stay home, had a new car, and lived in a lovely home. My husband was a wonderful man, and I had a great life, yet I could think of nothing. I finally said, "He walks our dog." My husband had given me a dog for Christmas, and he walked him every morning.

I awoke for my prayer time that first morning and slipped out of bed. I quietly left the room and closed the door behind me. The dog began to bark and scratch at the door. My husband called out, "Where are you?" I replied, "I'm praying." So he got out of bed and dutifully took care of the dog.

The next day, the same thing happened. This time my husband asked, "What are you doing?"

"I'm *praying*," I said, this time a little more emphatically.

"For the whole world?" he asked in frustration. Again, he got out of bed and took care of the dog.

On the third day I awoke and started to slip out of the room. Once again the dog began to scratch the door and bark to be taken outside. *What is the big deal here?* I thought to myself, *I'll walk the dog before praying.*

A bit grudgingly, I took the dog outside. I still remember the beauty of that early morning. The sky was magnificent, and the

264

moon cast shadows about me. I'm not sure I had ever seen the stars in the early morning before. The birds were chirping. It was a new day, and I was so thankful to be a part of it. The cool air stirred my soul. As I walked to the end of the driveway, I noticed the newspaper lying there.

I thought, "Why don't I take him the newspaper, along with a cup of coffee?" So I did. This seemingly insignificant choice was the beginning of my developing a new heart of love for my husband and receiving an overwhelming supply of love from him. I had chosen to serve him. In doing so, I had chosen to serve the Lord as well.

I felt so happy. Joy and contentment flooded my soul. I knew without a doubt that I was in a place of blessing from the Lord.

Had I not chosen to walk the dog, I never would have experienced the beauty of the morning or noticed the newspaper lying in the driveway. I wouldn't have picked it up or thought about taking my husband a cup of coffee.

Who would have thought that such a small, seemingly inconsequential thing would change my marriage so radically? Yet it did, because it began the change in me.

## CHANGE STARTS WITH YOU

Is your marriage in need of change? Perhaps it has been so cold for so long that it seems hopelessly frozen. But it's not! Can you begin to see that, regardless of how you've conducted yourself in your marriage before, now it's time to conduct yourself "as unto the Lord"?

Perhaps this is disheartening news to you. You may not be ready to treat your husband in this manner, yet you can no longer justify your current treatment of him. What are you called to do in such a case? You are called to be obedient to God's Word, regardless of your feelings towards you husband.

No doubt, there are many times in your marriage when your husband has made mistakes. Perhaps he has hurt your feelings, made an error in judgment, or been unduly harsh with you or the children. When this happens, it is natural to feel that he doesn't deserve to be treated well. Your tendency might be to withdraw or to lash out at him.

But the real issue isn't how your husband deserves to be treated, *but how Jesus deserves to be treated*. This makes it so simple! And it is motivating as well.

When you treat your husband coldly, it's as if Jesus Christ is right there with you, and you are treating Him coldly, too. This puts things in a completely different perspective. The way you're serving Christ, right now—today—is a direct reflection of the way you're serving your husband. *In fact, it's been said that your present relationship with your husband is a spiritual barometer of your relationship with Christ.* The Lord notices your efforts and promises a reward for your faithful service.

### An Inheritance from the Lord

One of the great promises of God is that He will reward you for the work you do as a sincere expression of your devotion to Him. *He notices what you do!* We cannot overstate this fact. Don't look to your husband to reward you for your ministry to him. God will do this!

There is a present reward—you will experience His presence and His power through the Holy Spirit. The supernatural outcome of this is fruit bearing.

There is a future reward as well as a present reward. There will be a time in eternity when you will be rewarded by Christ. He will give you crowns.

1. A crown that lasts forever. (1 Corinthians 9:25)
2. A crown of exultation. (1 Thessalonians 2:19)
3. A crown of righteousness. (2 Timothy 4:8)
4. The Conqueror's crown of glory. (1 Peter 5:4)
5. A crown of gold. (Revelation 4:4)

How wonderful to have crowns to lay at His nail-pierced feet. What else would we have to give Him? After all, we have nothing to boast of as we serve Him because anything done *for* Him is enabled *by* Him.

### Ministering to a Difficult Husband

Perhaps you have a husband who is distant toward you, and you are battling resignation and discouragement. Perhaps your husband is outright cold or mean-spirited and frequently puts you down. It is especially important for you to serve your husband "as unto the Lord" during those times and not slip back into believing that your husband's response determines your actions. It is helpful to remember that your *will*, not your *feelings*, determines your actions. This doesn't mean that your feelings of hurt or rejection will automatically disappear—they won't. It means, though, that you are choosing to serve God regardless of your husband's behavior. Fervently seek God during those times and ask Him to heal the wounds you bear.

We know of a woman whose husband constantly blamed her

for their poor marriage, even though it appeared she was working at it with all her heart. What did she do? She prayed even more fervently for her husband and her marriage and asked God to give her the strength to serve her husband as she would Him. And she boldly asked Him to enable her to do it in a joyful manner. "My hope is that my marriage will eventually change. But my greater hope is that I can one day stand before the Lord and have Him say to me, 'Well done, thy good and faithful servant. You were faithful to the end.'"

It's easy in the dailyness of life to get out of focus. This is especially true if you have a husband who is not responding to your efforts. God knows what is happening. Although at times He may seem far away, He is not. He is right there, closer than the beat of your heart, waiting to comfort and encourage you. He sees every action, hears every word, notes every hurt. He sees you pushing on as the storm rages around you, *and He does not forget it.* Scripture assures us of that.

This may be all that you have to hold on to. Remember that your heavenly Father will one day look at you and reward you for your godly behavior. Your heartache and pain will be erased forever, and you will receive an inheritance like no other—a royal inheritance given to you personally by Jesus Christ.

Does your motive need to change? Doing so is just a choice away.

## THE HUSBAND PARAPHRASE

We thought it would be fitting to end this chapter with our paraphrase of Matthew 25:35–40.

*I was hungry for breakfast, dinner,*
*and sometimes even lunch, snacks, a*
*kind word, a warm hug, to talk to you, to be loved by you...*
*...you gave me something to eat.*
*I was thirsty to feel accepted by you,*
*to take the leadership role in our*
*home, to be admired by you, to be respected by you.*
*I mowed the lawn and needed refreshing and...*
*...you gave me something to drink.*
*I was a stranger; my mood was bad.*
*I had been unreasonable.*
*I had been mean, thoughtless, forgetful, unhelpful, self-centered...*
*...you invited me in.*
*I was naked, you did all my wash*
*even when I dropped it on the floor.*
*You sewed on my missing buttons.*
*You let me bare my soul to you.*
*You ironed my wrinkled shirts.*
*You saw the real me that others never see—*
*with all my quirks and uncovered ugliness, and you never*
*exposed me before our children, family, or friends...*
*...you clothed me.*
*I was sick—you know my colds are worse than anyone else's.*
*Sometimes I said things to you I didn't mean. I got depressed and...*
*...you cared for me.*
*I was in prison: my job got to me some days and I withdrew from you.*
*When I was lonely you were there for me.*
*You prayed for me.*
*When I was consumed with a problem,*

*when I was unforgiving, when I didn't deserve*
*anything because of the way I've treated you and I was so ashamed...*
*...you came to me.*
*Jesus would say to you, "When you did these things for your*
*husband, you did them for Me."*

*Press on!* An inheritance from the Lord awaits you.

*Press on!* Can't you hear the trumpets sounding? The heavens applauding? Can't you imagine the misting of your eyes as they meet the sweet soft gaze of His? Can't you sense the swelling of your heart and the joyful singing of your soul as He wraps His loving arms around you and says, "Well done"?

*Oh, dear reader, press on!* As you serve your husband, you serve the King of kings and Lord of lords! Your efforts are of great worth to Him!

## CHAPTER 9 SUMMARY

1.  Unless a woman's motive for her marriage lines up with God's plan, fulfillment and satisfaction will elude her.

2.  As you serve your husband, you are actually serving Jesus Christ.

3.  Serving your husband "as unto the Lord" brings joy and peace.

4.  Whatever you do, you are to work at it with all your heart.

5.  The Lord always rewards obedience.

6.  Don't look to your husband to reward you for your ministry. Jesus promises to reward you Himself.

7.  Serving a difficult husband doesn't mean you won't have feelings of hurt or rejection. It means, though, that you are choosing to be obedient to God's Word even in the midst of difficulty.

# Part 6

# The Results

Every woman's marriage is different, and there is something to be learned from every story. As you read the following pages, experience the amazing power of God at work in lives that are surrendered to Him.

You will see hardened hearts softened, stubborn wills remolded, and contentious spirits released. You will also see that not every story ends happily, from our perspective, but that God will continue to pour out His blessings on those faithful to Him.

As these women chronicle their experiences, it is our hope that you will be inspired to walk more closely with God—not only in your marriage, but in everyday life. This is what it's really all about! What a wonderful thing it is to choose obedience to Christ! These women have done just that. We salute them and praise God for their choices!

*Triumphs and Testimonies...to God be the glory!*

# CHAPTER TEN

# Triumphs and Testimonies

*It is no small thing when a woman chooses God's way over her own.*

## STANDING IN AWE

My husband and I were both raised in Christian homes and grew up in evangelical churches. We were educated at a Christian college. We loved God and felt we had a firm grasp of the Christian life. We were ready to live "happily ever after," and, because of our solid Christian background, felt well equipped to do so.

Our marriage began with a solid understanding of what it takes to have a close relationship, yet we found ourselves struggling to keep it on good terms. When you get married, you quickly discover that the nice person that you thought you were somehow disappears as you deal with the pressures of home, work, children, and relationships. After twenty years of marriage, we found ourselves avoiding each other. We didn't want to spend time together because we usually started picking at each other, until one or both of us became hurt. We would then retreat into our own silent worlds, the ever widening chasm growing even larger. Some of our closest friends were struggling openly in their marriages, and we became frightened that we were headed down the same slippery slope. We didn't want this. We didn't want our family life destroyed, our boys' hearts torn apart, or the sacred commitment we had made before God and man reduced to nothing more than a hollow shell. We knew we had to work on our relationship.

I wasn't sure what to do, but I knew we needed help; the life was being sucked out of our relationship. I was concerned not only for our marriage, but about the example we were setting for of our sons. How would they ever know what a godly relationship was like from our behavior? We were teaching them what *not* to do in marriage, and this alarmed both my husband and me.

I began learning about the principles in this book and soon discovered it wasn't our activities that were killing our relationship. But pride, selfishness, and sin were.

This is when I invited Christ back into my marriage and asked Him to help me be the wife He wanted me to become. Almost

*"When you get married, you quickly discover that the nice person you thought you were somehow disappears."*

instantly God began working in my heart and convicting me of sinful attitudes in my life. Once I realized that I wasn't treating and regarding my husband in a godly manner, the changes came rather easily. No one was more surprised about this than I, for I am the typical modern day woman who is used to running the show at home. I don't like change unless it's my idea. So I was amazed to see myself changing so readily.

An example of this was an evening when my husband and I had planned to attend a fund-raising dinner. As the dinner hour approached, my husband had yet to arrive home. Being late for an event is one of my pet peeves, and in the past I would get upset when this happened and vent my frustrations the moment he walked in the door.

But God was working in my life. I had asked Him to help me change, and He was! When my husband arrived home, I greeted him warmly and asked about his day. He briefly told me and then asked if I still wanted to attend the dinner, considering the time and my penchant for punctuality.

"What would you like to do?" I responded, "Do you feel like going, or are you too tired? Whatever you want to do is fine with me." To my amazement, I meant every word I spoke.

"I feel fine," my husband said, "let's go to the dinner."

So we went and had a wonderful time. Never once did I say, "Where were you?" "Why weren't you on time?" or "You know how crazy it makes me to be late."

On the way home, my husband looked at me and said, "You know, you're changing. I'm not sure what it is, but you're changing. When you allowed me to make the choice and didn't dictate what we'd do, you put the responsibility on my shoulders where it belonged. You didn't shame me, and you didn't push your will on me. You allowed me to lead and I like that."

God helped me to stop mothering my husband and become the wife my husband needed. My husband loves it! I am complete and fulfilled as I submit to being a wife to my husband. Before, I knew *intellectually* that I was responsible for my behavior, as my husband was for his, but now I believe it with my whole heart and try to live it.

I'm constantly amazed at how much my husband loves me when I allow him to—when I stop nagging and picking at him and step into the role God meant for me to fill. I'm always totally overwhelmed at the results.

The principles laid out in Scripture for being a godly wife are clear. I asked God to help me change and show me how to treat my husband differently, lovingly, respectfully. God has been faithful. As I have lined up my behavior with God's Word, my husband has responded by loving and cherishing me more than ever before in our marriage. I believe that God changes men's hearts "without words by the behavior of their wives." *I believe this principle is true whether a man is a believer or not.*

We all have different problems in our relationships. My issues will not be yours. But I can encourage you with joyful confidence to commit your marriage to the Lord. Invite Him into your marriage and be willing to be the one to change. Listen to what He tells you—obey His commands. You'll stand in awe of how He can work in your life when you do this. *When you're obedient to God, you're the beneficiary.* I give God the praise for what He has done in my marriage.

## REMOVING THE MASK

Many people are surprised to discover that I have a voice, for I am generally known to sit back and observe. I try to remind myself of the proverb, "Even a fool is thought wise if he keeps silent, and discerning if he holds his tongue" (Proverbs 17:28, NIV). However, I am an entirely different person at home.

For background, my family emigrated from Scotland when I was one year old. The Scottish are known for their feuding clans. My mother always said that my dad's family could pick a fight in an empty house. I believe I inherited that trait. My father was an alcoholic and verbally abusive. My mom kept the ship afloat, while my dad lowered the boom. We moved frequently, and I attended eleven schools. I still was unable to read by the time I was in sixth grade. I was, and still am, a slow learner in many ways.

I became a Christian at age sixteen. My dad died when I was twenty-one. Such freedom! I began to change. I came out of my shell, but I put on a mask of self-confidence. A year before my dad's death, I became engaged to a non-Christian much like my dad. An hour before the wedding, I called it off. I knew I belonged to God and couldn't go through with it. Three years later I married a man who met my requirements: a Christian, handsome, intelligent, noncontrolling, nonconfrontational, and patient. My husband waited twenty-nine years for me. But he didn't know what he was getting—although I once told him, "I don't know if you're strong enough for me."

I love the movie, *Mary Poppins*, especially the part where she measures herself—*almost perfect*. That's how I thought of myself. I expected perfection in myself and others. Nothing my husband did was right or good enough. I ridiculed my husband for having feelings and being emotional. When he brought home flowers for our one-month anniversary, I criticized him for how much he spent. When we went out of town for a weekend, I cried because we stayed at a $60.00 a night hotel instead of one that cost just $29.00 a night. When we bought our first house, I wouldn't let him carry me over the threshold—"What would the neighbors say?" I didn't know how to handle love.

*"When you are obedient to God, you are the beneficiary."*

My husband usually didn't react quickly enough to situations, so I easily usurped the authority in our home. I paid the bills and oversaw the care and discipline of the children. When he wanted to talk to me, I had to straighten the kitchen or take care of the children. In other words, I had no time for him. I didn't like getting beneath the surface. I was uncomfortable. I liked my mask.

Twenty years ago I was in a Bible study where we were told to let our husbands lead. I laughed out loud. But I noticed no one else laughed. Never before had I heard anything so ridiculous. I said to myself, "If he wants to lead, he's going to have to fight for it."

So here I am still in control after almost twenty-five years of marriage. Since the beginning of this year, God has put the desire of Psalm 51:10 and 12b in me: "Create in me a pure heart, O God, and renew a steadfast spirit within me…. And grant me a willing spirit…."

As a result of the teaching in this book, I became restless. At a recent women's retreat, the question was asked, "What does glorifying God look like in your daily life?" There was also a special song at the retreat which spoke of glorifying God. That really troubled me. What does it mean to glorify God? What am I supposed to do? When I got home, I looked up the definitions of "glory" and "glorify." I looked up verses with those words in them. I was very troubled. I read in Proverbs: "If you call out for insight and cry aloud for understanding, and if you look for it as for silver and search for it as for hidden treasure, then you will understand the fear of the Lord and find the knowledge of God" (Proverbs 2:3–4, NIV).

Finally, it became clear: *Obedience is the answer!* Before Jesus went to the cross, He said, "I have brought you glory on earth by completing the work you gave me to do" (John 17:4, NIV). What was the work that God gave Him? "He humbled Himself and became obedient to death" (Philippians 2:8, NIV). God is so patient with me! Now what do I do? Psalm 119:60 says, "I will hasten and not delay to obey your commands."

So I decided to start obeying His commands in this whole area, and I noticed a difference almost immediately. I have shocked my husband by asking for his opinion *and abiding by it.* I now take time to sit and listen to him. He has twenty-five years of stuffed things to say! I've set the scene for some romantic encounters at home. He even suggested that I buy a bikini and we go away for a weekend. I have never worn a bikini in my life, and he hasn't suggested we get away since the hotel incident over twenty years ago.

I read somewhere that frequently when people are talking about how they are struggling through something, what they really mean is that they are putting off obedience. I hope you don't delay for twenty years like I did.

Finally, a quote from Karen Burton Main's book, *Karen, Karen*: "My husband should become my chief ministry. My prayers are for him. My insight for him. Love of Christ within me, for him. Lie beside his sleeping form at night and pray, pray for his preservation, pray for the building up of his depleted spiritual forces. It was only after I began to grow deeply spiritual that I realized [my husband] had been ahead of me all the time. Too long he had stood alone guarding against the onslaught. One regret [of Karen and also mine] is: I didn't answer my summons to spiritual growth sooner. I dallied so long. It is essential that I grow quickly because I am to be [my husband's] burden-bearer."[1]

My husband and I had a quiet celebration of our twenty-fifth wedding anniversary. We went away for a weekend alone—twenty years after the original disaster we were trying it again! Yes, I did buy a bikini! I packed it in my suitcase. But I vacillated on whether to get it out or go with my old tried-and-true swimsuit. I donned my new bikini and covered it up on the way to the pool. After all, *people* were there! But I plunged into the pool anyway. My husband was so pleased that I had honored his request. He had hoped that I would, but, knowing how self-conscious I am, didn't really expect to see me in a bikini.

On the day of our anniversary, I purchased a large floral arrangement of blue carnations and white daisies, just like we had for our wedding day. I chose not to have them delivered (to save the delivery fee, of course). After picking them up, I tried to avoid taking them to his office, as I had planned on just taking them home for him to enjoy when he returned from work. I had to keep repeating 2 Chronicles 16:9: "The eyes of the Lord range through-out the earth to strengthen those whose hearts are fully committed to Him." I really needed strengthening then. My desire is to be fully committed to God and to my husband. God granted me strength, and I delivered the flowers to his office. My husband was filled with pleasure.

These two simple acts—buying the bikini and delivering him flowers—represented a softened heart. I was saying, "Let's begin again; I'm your 'new' old wife!"

At last, I have a teachable spirit. The time has come for tossing away my mask!

## A CHANGED HEART

Twenty years ago, a marriage began. With it began a tug-of-war for control of the home.

Our first battle was over the issue of submission. My fiancé's brother, who held a doctorate in theology, was going to speak at our wedding. He discussed with us his plan to speak on the husband's responsibility to be head of the marriage and the wife's responsibility to submit to her husband. I threw a first-class fit. I couldn't believe he was serious. After many tears and hurt feelings and no regard for God's truth, I convinced my soon-to-be brother-in-law to tone down his message. But my opinion remained unchanged.

In 1978, submission wasn't a popular cultural view. Nor is it today. I was inundated with claims that a woman had as much right to headship in the home as the man did. Not only did I agree, I felt sure I could do the better job. *My pride ranneth over.*

Shortly after that time, we moved to a nearby city where my husband began his medical schooling and residency training. This took nine years—nine *long* years. He was basically absent—mentally, emotionally, and physically. Whenever he was home, he was exhausted. The leadership role was mine for the taking, and I was more than happy to assume it. I wanted it no other way.

I made all the decisions in the relationship—major and minor. I ran the house, birthed two babies, and had total responsibility for their care. My husband came home, often in the middle of the night, and left again before the sun came up. He was doing what was expected of a medical student and surgery resident. Whenever my husband *was* home, I secretly felt that he was in my way.

*In 1978, submission wasn't a popular cultural view. Nor is it today.*

One day he came home and announced that he had decided to change residency programs. I was shocked, but to my amazement, I found myself getting excited about the idea—maybe we would see more of him now.

And we did. A lot more. *Too much more.* The battle for control started again. He was infringing on my territory. I felt I had done a good job and was none too eager to share the leadership with him. I had no intention of letting it go.

After ten years of marriage, God began to work on me little by little. Believe it or not, up to this point my husband and I enjoyed a great relationship because I got to make the decisions and generally get my way. Who wouldn't be happy with this arrangement? But I became seriously ill after our youngest son was born. I was sick for virtually two and a half years. Several surgeries later, which culminated in a hysterectomy due to endometriosis, I was, for the first time in our marriage, unable to run things.

My husband took over out of necessity. He did everything. *Everything.* Laundry. Cooking. Baby care. Toddler care. Invalid wife care. He cleaned, shopped, mopped, scrubbed, and loved. He saved me. He loved me unconditionally and took care of me totally. When he was at work, he hired a nanny and a housecleaner to do what he couldn't. All he wanted was for me to get well. I cherish forever the memory of how he became Christ to me during that time and in the ensuing years. He is more precious to me today than I can even begin to say.

My heart began to change. I found God speaking to me on the subject of submission in all areas of my life to Him and to my husband as well.

When I first received the teachings in this book, my eyes and heart were ready, eager to learn what God wanted from me and for me. I began to see that I was protected by my husband's covering of responsibility before the Lord. He was to submit to the Lord and love me as his wife. I was to submit to my husband as unto the Lord. What a thought! I was excited as I began putting these principles to work in my life.

I began by giving over control of major decisions to my husband. One example is in the area of money. I had always done our taxes, insurance, bills, and taken care of the checkbook. My husband wanted to be involved in this, so I gave it back to him, giving my opinion when he asked it. What a surprise it was to him to discover that he had the final say in the matter. It is amazing to me how he embraced the role of leader, once I let go of it. Had I not let go, I feel certain he would have continued letting me run things just to keep some semblance of peace within our home.

I tried to submit in all areas of our marriage, even in the bedroom.

A newly discovered joy and sweetness entered our marriage that had never been there before.

I can say, with conviction and confidence, that God is blessing us beyond measure. Our marriage has become fun. Fun! At one time this seemed like a foreign concept to us. I no longer shoulder the responsibilities. My husband wants them and does a wonderful job fulfilling them. He has become my provider, lover, best friend. We would rather spend time together than with anyone else.

I grieve for the years that were lost, but I thank God that they are no more. I thank Him that my eyes were opened and that He caused my heart to soften toward His Word and towards my role as a wife. After twenty years, we are looking forward to the best years ahead of us, God willing.

*It is amazing to me how he embraced the role of leader, once I let go of it.*

Every now and then the issue of control surfaces still. This usually happens when I am out of God's Word. Once I go back to it, He always helps me return to my rightful spot within my marriage.

I cannot say how thankful I am to have been blessed by the teachings in this book to learn what my role is as a wife, to fulfill my God-given job description, and for the role models I've had along the way. I hope one day to be such a model for others.

God's Word works! *It's the secret to a wonderful marriage.* My prayer for all readers is that they would come to know God and experience the transformation that comes from walking in obedience.

## BEAUTY FROM ASHES

Twelve years ago, my husband and I moved to a new city. Prior to that, we had been separated for nearly a year. We weren't really happy together, but realized a reconciliation had to at least be attempted for the children's sake. At that time, there was no congeniality in our home. What there was, though, was a great deal of hostility and animosity. Rarely a day went by without fighting or violent outbursts. We coped in our individual ways: both my husband and I began drinking more and more heavily to lessen the mental turmoil that existed in our home; worse than that, our teenage daughter began using drugs.

My husband and I started looking for ways to show our children what a family was supposed to look like. We began attending church again. It was at that time that I began learning about the principles in this book. My first thought was that I didn't need any teaching on being a wife, *my husband needed teaching on being a husband!*

As I began learning my job description as a wife, big changes began to happen. I was so surprised! The Lord reached into my heart and shook it up. I discovered that I was the one who needed to change, and I learned why I needed to—to be obedient to God's Word. However, those changes didn't begin until after I accepted Christ into my life. Once I did, the changes occurred by leaps and bounds. I learned that submission to my husband was God's idea, and it was pleasing to Him.

*My husband shared that because of how much I had changed, he knew God had to be powerful.*

I also learned that God would forgive me if only I asked. How I wanted forgiveness! I wrote a long letter to God and included everything I felt I needed forgiveness for. Then I wrote down everything I felt I needed to forgive my husband for. I asked God to forgive me for being angry and promised to forgive my husband, as He had forgiven me. I claimed a verse as I did this: Matthew 6:14–15: "For if you forgive men when they sin against you, your heavenly Father will also forgive you. But if you do not forgive men their sins, your Father will not forgive your sins." After a notebook of writing, a bucket of tears, and a box of Kleenex, I felt like a new person. I knew, beyond a shadow of a doubt, that I had recommitted my life to the Lord that day.

I began building my husband up. He was shocked and didn't know what to make of it. I had always been *destructive* to his ego, not *constructive*. It was challenging for me at first, as old habits die hard, but as I began to build him up, he began to treat me better as well. He kept asking me why I was doing this. I would respond that I was doing it because it pleased God.

We continued to worship together and decided to become members of the church. During the membership class, we were not completely confident in our answers to all of the questions: "If you were to die today, do you know for sure that you'd go to heaven?" "What would you say to Christ as to why He should let you into heaven?" Through this class, one of the pastors invited us to attend a series he was beginning. We said yes, and during a sharing time, we were asked how we came to know the Lord. I was shocked when my husband said he began to study the Bible because of the changes he saw in my life. I was completely surprised. I had no idea this had happened. My husband shared that because of how much

I had changed, he knew God had to be powerful. He said he loved the way I changed and could see as well how God continued working in my life. Again, Scripture came to mind: 1 Peter 3:1–2 (NIV): "Wives, in the same way be submissive to your husbands so that, if any of them do not believe the Word, they may be won over without words by the behavior of their wives, when they see the purity and reverence of your lives."

As our lives continued to change, so did our children. They began attending church, and though we had to push them at first, before long they didn't want to miss it! The Holy Spirit has patched a lot of wounds and forgiveness has overshadowed much grief and hurt.

I pray that this testimony can cause others to see that God is living and powerful and touches every aspect of our lives. He is always waiting to have a relationship with us if only we ask Him. God is alive and touches lives. When I became obedient to His Word, my life was changed. With all of my heart I thank Him and those He used to do this. Our home is becoming more of a haven every day. What a joy this is. My hope is that this would happen in your home, too.

## A WIFE'S REWARD

Audrey is a beautiful woman who loves the Lord. She was married for forty-three years to a difficult man who was an alcoholic. Her husband recently died, but a week prior to his death, he received Jesus as his Savior. We asked her about this, and she told us how she had tried to be her husband's Holy Spirit for years, to no avail. Several years ago, she decided that she would begin to pray for her husband with a group of faithful Christian women. She stopped trying to control and change her husband and, instead, began praying for him. Her husband began to soften ever so slightly, and occasionally he went to Sunday school social events. It wasn't until he was stricken with a terminal disease that he was spiritually open.

A week before he died, a pastor from her church visited. The pastor asked her husband if he knew for sure whether he would go to heaven when he died. The pastor offered to tell him how people can be sure they had eternal life. He agreed. As the pastor shared this, the man's eyes never left his face. Once he finished, he asked Audrey's husband if he would like to pray and trust Jesus as his Lord and Savior. He said yes.

A week later, he became much weaker. It was a gray day, and Audrey was sitting beside his bed, holding his hand. She turned to look out the window. As she did so, two clouds parted, and a rainbow formed behind them. She turned to her husband and told him she felt this was the day that he would be in heaven with Jesus. A tear slid down his face. A short time later, he died.

The day following the memorial service, she and her son noticed that beside his chair was a yellow legal pad. She picked it up and out dropped a folded piece of paper. On it was written a tribute to Audrey. This is what it said:

*My Angel*
   "angel"—one of an order of spiritual beings that are attendants and messengers of God—

> *My Angel:*
> *—held me, prayed for me, and suffered with*

*me during those indescribable pain periods.*
*—held and consoled me when emotions just made me want to cry.*
*—virtually put her life on hold to take care of mine.*
*Handled every aspect of my needs. Constantly "on call."*
*THANK YOU, GOD, for giving me My Angel.*
*Actually she's a Living Angel.*
*I call her...........Audrey.*

We asked Audrey, "Was it worth being in a difficult marriage for forty-three years, knowing now that the outcome was that your husband came to know Christ without a word from you?"

"Although some of the memories are difficult still, as I look back over the years, it was worth it, and I thank God for revealing to me the importance of 1 Peter 3:1: 'Wives, in the same way be submissive to your husbands so that, if any of them do not believe the word, they may be won over without words by the behavior of their wives.' It was *so* worth it."

## FAITHFULNESS IN THE MIDST OF THE STORM

I was married for twenty-five years. My marriage experienced stormy times, several to the point of divorce. We had renewed our vows to each other and to Christ in 1992, and it was a glorious time and a tremendous testimony of Christ's healing.

After two years, workaholism and drivenness resurfaced in my husband. He once again became tired, distant, and angry. Old sins sometimes die hard, and I sensed there may have been another woman.

A godly friend encouraged me to pursue my husband as I did

when I was dating him. My task was to observe him and do things I knew he would like. I did everything from preparing for his nightly shower with clean towels, underwear, and love notes, to renting a limousine and picking him up from work in style. I tried all I knew to show him I loved and cared for him. When someone works until late at night, you must get creative in how to serve.

> *My husband's response was minimal.*
>
> *My Savior's response was great.*

My friend took it one step further and began coming to my home to teach me one-on-one about God's Word and what He says about marriage. I kept asking, "Why am I doing this?" and "What about him?" Through the Word and the examples in this book, I finally began to realize what I was to do. It was what God called me to do. It became an obedience issue.

My husband continued down his path and grew more distant. There was little I could do to reach him. I ministered to him nightly through gentle back massages. Many nights I was angry and wanted to lash out. I kept silent and continued on my *mission to minister*. As I would begin to rub his back, it was almost as if I could feel the Lord's hand on mine. My husband's response was minimal. My Savior's response was great.

I'd like to say he turned around as he had before, but he did not. He divorced me, left the state, and soon remarried.

What was the point of trying? My situation is not easy, but God has honored my obedience to Him. I have peace knowing I was obedient to God's Word. My children have "risen up and called me blessed," because they knew I did what was right in the eyes of God. My oldest daughter said, "Mom, you didn't drive him out, righteousness did. Darkness can't tolerate the light and you were the light."

I would say to wives who are frustrated and wanting to leave their marriages: *Don't ever give up!* You have a choice as to how you will respond in your marriage. You cannot control your spouse. You can only control you. Let go of *him* and keep your eyes on *Him*. I have experienced both the resurrection of a marriage and the death of a marriage. Never give up! There is great pain in divorce. It can seem worse than death. If you walk away, you will be responsible before God. Not only do you cause yourself pain, but there is great pain for your children. Instead, choose to be obedient and join hands with God in resurrecting something. Your marriage! In spite of how you feel right now, you can do it. Keep your eyes on Him, obey His commands for marriage, and no matter what response you get, you can be satisfied because you chose love and obedience.

## STREAMS IN THE WASTELAND

Our marriage was in a coma, and it had been for most of our twenty-six years together. It wasn't dead yet, but certainly the coma was profound and deep. There was no feeling, no communication, no interaction. Even the pain was removed, leaving just a numbness—a sort of mere existence.

Our coma was induced not by a severe blow, though we had experienced the death of our infant daughter, unemployment, and teens in rebellion. Instead, it was brought on by the small injuries of hurts, resentments, grudges, bitterness, and the real killer of unforgiveness. We were being kept alive by various support systems: our commitment to stay married, praying friends, and knowing God would not let us go. There was a faint "bleep" on the monitor that showed our union was not yet dead. The "bleep" was faith—as small as a mustard seed.

We brought excess baggage into our marriage—much of it was shame and regret from our courtship days that seemed relentless in destroying whatever repentance and newness came from our new lives in Christ. We had both accepted Christ during our seventh year of marriage and sincerely desired to honor Him with it. We would succeed for a time and then fail for an even longer time. From the outside, we fooled many people. We became involved in Christian service, even assuming leadership roles. I held key leadership roles in women's ministries for four years, my husband was involved in worship leadership for six and was even considered for eldership during that time. Our church masks were firmly in place, and our pride kept them there.

But the coma was deepening. Our ministries had become powerless and our prayer life ineffective. My husband twice experienced job loss, and our family was self-destructing. Each of our three teenage children was going through various stages of anger and rebellion. How big a price were we willing to pay for our cherished sins of pride and unforgiveness?

We wanted things to change. We finally confided in our closest friends and family. They prayed fervently. Over a six-year period we went to three different pastors for counseling. We finally sought a professional counselor and spent over sixteen hundred dollars in three months. Nothing was improving—in fact, the situation was worsening. Both a friend and a family member advised me to leave my husband, at least temporarily. I was ready. We were all unhappy. All but one.

Satan was overjoyed. He was sensing victory. Somehow, we had given him a foothold. I don't know exactly when this occurred, but it was a day long ago when we had hurt one another and chosen unforgiveness. This continued into the next day...and the next...and the next. Before we knew it, it stretched into a week...a month...a year...a way of life.

John 8:44 reminds us that Satan "is a liar and the father of lies." I believed this and began considering what lies my mind was listening to:

"You can never overcome the baggage of sin,
   guilt, shame, lack of trust."
      "Your marriage was doomed from the beginning..."
      "Why not get out and find some happiness..."
         "You deserve better..."
            "It is hopeless..."
               "He's a jerk..."

Satan, the liar, the deceiver, had managed to convince me that my husband was the enemy.

A year ago at a family life conference, I learned that "the family is God's smallest battlefield, and Satan is the enemy." I saw that Satan had almost gained the victory in our marriage by convincing me that my husband was the enemy. Oh, he could never reclaim us for his own, or snatch our salvation from us, but we had been gripped by such a spirit of despair that we were rendered powerless.

Our prayers were ineffective because we were cherishing sin in our hearts. We refused to come to God with "clean hands and a pure heart." The pain of our pride was destroying our marriage, but that same pride kept us from surrendering and forgiving.

Then, finally, suddenly, we began awakening from the coma. God was at work. Our interceding friends had been so faithful. I knew the Holy Spirit had come alongside us to convict us of our need to confess, repent, and forgive one another. We talked to each other…we *listened*. The last thing my husband said while I was in the final stages of resistance was, "I have to remember that you're not the enemy!" That did it. The deceiver was revealed. The father of lies was seen for who he really is. We chose to confess our pride, along with numerous other sins, and to apologize and forgive. Hallelujah!

We are new at this. We realize that we could fail again tomorrow. But God reassures us with these words from Isaiah 43:18–19: "Forget the former things, do not dwell on the past. See, I am doing a new thing! I am making a way in the desert and streams in the wasteland… that they may proclaim My praise."

I implore you not to make the same mistake I did. I learned of the principles in this book long ago, but I resisted them. These principles aren't the key to change. *Your obedience is.* You can know these principles forward and backward, but you will be rendered powerless, as I was, until you choose to act on them. Don't waste your life disobeying God's Word…*let it be used for His glory.*

# Chapter 11: A Speechless Husband Speaks

What could be worse than to never be first in the heart of your precious bride?

What could be harder than to have son or daughter take your place and push you aside?

What could be dearer than to be loved and nearer your wife than all others combined?

# A Speechless Husband Speaks

*How very blessed is the man who has a wife who walks with God.*

**I**t is a privilege to write of God's great work in our marriage. The principles taught in this book have changed my wife, our marriage, and have changed my life almost beyond belief.

For background information, I tend to be a perfectionist, and as a newlywed, I had a certain idea of what marriage should be like. My expectations were high—high for myself, for the marriage, and certainly for my wife. She was a great spouse, who did her best to make our marriage a good one, but my expectations were so high that in my eyes she often fell short. Coupled with this, I was in an intense training program, where I was constantly pressured, stressed, and exhausted.

Unfortunately, as the early years went by, I didn't learn to soften my expectations much, and my wife grew weary and discouraged. She told me that she finally came to the conclusion that even though she had tried so hard, since it didn't seem to make a difference, why keep trying?

To make a long story short, we both began to grow cold. We developed a certain hopelessness in our marriage, and an overwhelming pain and emptiness entered our home.

After a number of years, I began realizing that a great deal of what had occurred in our marriage was due to my perfectionistic attitude. I wanted to change, but by this time, my wife had grown distant and was filled with resentment. It seemed that now any efforts I made were not enough. I was reaping what I had sown.

Our marriage seemed to be a constant battleground—over almost any issue, big or small. If I felt one way, she looked at it differently. I wanted to be respected as a husband and be the leader of the home; she gave me neither. She wanted to be unconditionally loved and cherished; I gave her neither.

A few years ago, we finally sat down together to try to repair our marriage. We were tired and unhappy. It no longer seemed to matter so much who was right and who was wrong. We knew, as we had all along, that our marriage wasn't the kind we had hoped to model for our children. We knew our ministry was limited because of it. But most importantly, we knew our marriage wasn't pleasing to God. In fact, it seemed in many ways a mockery to God. We committed ourselves to changing. And even though we had tried to change before, this time we began making some progress.

But the one thing that seemed to be consistently missing was joy in the marriage. We seemed to go about dutifully fulfilling our marital responsibilities, but there was no joy. However, we had lived in pain for so long we could survive without the joy, just so long as bitterness and anger were no longer the dominating forces.

> "She took her eyes off of me and put them on Christ, and that is where the change began."

A few years ago, my wife began living the principles in this book. I am conservative, and not prone to being overly dramatic, but, quite honestly, she was transformed. She literally became a different person in many areas of her life. Anger was replaced with kindness, pride with humility, and opposition with respect. She developed the sincere desire to serve and respect me as her husband. And she seemed to burn with a desire to serve and obey God in a way that she never had before.

I began seeing a newness in my wife—in the way she talked, in the way she spoke to me, in the way she responded to my requests, in the way she served me, and in the way she was willing to humble herself in an effort to be obedient to God. What I was seeing was Christ in her. So it was Christ who began changing my wife, and, in turn, it was the Christ in her that softened my own heart.

We still had (and have) our differences, of course, like any married couple. But I saw in my wife a willingness, almost eagerness, to make things right between herself and God, and as a result, things were made right between us. I'm sure if you asked her, she'd say there were lots of times she may not have felt I deserved any special treatment. But there was no doubt in her mind that God did. *She took her eyes off of me and put them on Christ, and that is where the change began.*

How has this transformation made me feel?

First of all, I feel much more free to be who I am because my wife is no longer sitting in constant judgment of me. If some of your husbands are like I was, I felt that no matter what I did, I was going to lose. I now feel like I have an advocate rather than an adversary in my wife. And this gives me a confidence that I hadn't had before.

I also feel affection for my wife. I know this probably sounds strange, but it is hard to show affection when there's a high likelihood that it will be rejected. Although affection was something she always wanted, it was something I always had a hard time giving, because of the constant battle between us. In the past, because of our struggles, we poured our affections into our children, and they became our priorities rather than each other. But now, our priorities have become each other, and affection for each other comes more naturally and freely. Our children love this!

I can tell you that all the men I know, including myself, desire respect more than love. If a man doesn't feel respected in his home, he not only feels undermined on issues in the home, he feels undermined as a man. I now feel respected by my wife. I now feel I am the leader of the home, and my wife's willingness to respect that title causes me to more freely seek her wisdom and counsel on issues. It has also caused me to respect *her* more deeply.

Another thing is that the hypocrisy that plagued me in past years is gone. The guilt at knowing that my personal life was a mess as I tried to maintain various ministries is gone. I no longer feel hindered as I approach God.

*We have rediscovered how invaluable humility is. It is the cornerstone of our marriage.*

I no longer dread coming home from work, wondering what the temperature will be when I walk through the door. For many men (and women, no doubt) there's a lot of pressure and stress during the workday. Most of us want a place to come home to where we are appreciated and accepted as we are. My wife used to tell me that she didn't worry about my feeling unappreciated because in her eyes I got that affirmation and acceptance at work. But for me, at least, when I experience acceptance at home, I am far better equipped to do well at work.

Fun and friendship have also reentered our marriage. We enjoy each other, do things together, and often just sit and talk, which we never used to do.

I feel far more peaceful. In the past, even in the good times, we knew that it was just a matter of time before things would deteriorate again. But now, even on our bad days, the foundation remains firm. We have rediscovered how invaluable humility is. It is one of the cornerstones of our marriage.

Finally, I feel excited—excited by the spiritual journey my wife is taking, excited by the spiritual insights we are gaining from one another, and excited by the spiritual intimacy we are beginning to experience.

So I guess if I could leave you with a final thought, it's this: My wife made a decision to honor God through *obedience* and committed, with His help, to apply biblical principles to our marriage. As a result of her decision, I feel God has given us a foundation that never was there before. She didn't focus on me, she focused on God. And the fruit of love, patience, forgiveness, and respect has entered our home.

I humbly share with you today that in our marriage, at least, our hope was rediscovered when my wife committed to being obedient to godly principles. That's not to say that I think the responsibility is more the wife's than the husband's, because I don't. We are all responsible for our actions. But I would encourage you not to wait for your husbands. Instead I would encourage you to start doing *now* what you know God has called you to do. I know for some of you, this may seem so hard—but don't wait. *God doesn't honor our waiting; He doesn't honor our intentions*—but He *does* honor our obedience.

I'd like to close with a section of Scripture that seems to capture the essence of these issues:

> "Therefore, since we are surrounded by such a great cloud of witnesses, let us throw off everything that hinders and the sin that so easily entangles, and let us run with perseverance the race marked out for us. *Let us fix our eyes on Jesus,* the author and perfecter of our faith, who for the joy set before him endured the cross, scorning its shame, and sat down at the right hand of the throne of God. *Consider him* who endured such opposition from sinful men, so that you will not grow weary and lose heart." (Hebrews 12:1, NIV, emphasis added)

May each of you reading this book fix your eyes on Jesus—consider Him—and in so doing, become who He made you to be.

# Epilogue

J ohn 2 tells about a wedding in Cana, where the host ran out of wine. Jesus' mother went to Him, knowing He could take care of it. He took water from six large jars and changed it into wine. The wine that had His touch upon it was far better than what had been served originally.

As we individually meditated on this verse, we noticed that Jesus accepted wedding invitations and that when His help was requested, He responded. So in the privacy of our own homes, we invited Him into our marriages, asking Him to fill what we had run out of:

hope...

joy...

desire...

peace...

love...

When we asked for His help, He gave it in overwhelming measure. As we began to follow His plan for us, we experienced His blessings as never before.

There are still days when we fail, but we know to Whom to turn. We sometimes slip back into questioning, "Did God really say....?" But we know He did! And we don't want to live our lives the old way ever again.

Would you consider inviting Jesus back into your marriage? Would you consider putting His Word to work in your life?

In his book *Strike the Original Match,* Charles Swindoll gives this warning:

> Let me mention one more "cheap substitute" so common among Christian wives in our day. It is learning about what's right rather than doing what is right... It has been my observation that a large percentage of Christian wives know more—much more—than they put into practice. And yet, they are continually interested in attending another class, taking another course, reading another book, going to another seminar... And what results?

Normally, greater guilt. Or on the other side, an enormous backlog of theoretical data that blinds and thickens the conscience rather than spurs it into action. Learning more truth is a poor and cheap substitute for stopping and putting into action the truth already learned.[1]

Knowledge isn't the answer, obedience is! Never would the ark have been built if Noah hadn't picked up that first piece of wood in obedience to God. Never would the Red Sea have been crossed if Moses hadn't taken that first step to lead his people into the Promised Land. Never would the great masterpieces of our time have been painted if the artist hadn't first dipped the paintbrush into the paint.

We challenge you to take that first step, as small as it might be, and begin a journey that will change your life forever! Remember, you're never alone. There is One traveling with you who never slumbers, sleeps, nor grows weary.

It is the dearest thing to place your life in the hands of God and say, "Lord, change me." Would you consider doing this today?

# NOTES

CHAPTER 1

1. Ed Wheat, *Love Life for Every Married Couple* (Zondervan Publishing House, Grand Rapids, Mich., 1980), 61.

CHAPTER 2

1. Susan T. Foh, *Women and the Word of God: A Response to Biblical Feminism* (Phillipsburg, N.J: Presbyterian and Reformed Publishing Co., 1979), 69.
2. *The Billy Graham Christian Worker's Handbook* (Minneapolis, MN: Worldwide Publishers, 1984), 5–6.
3. Frank B. Minirth and Paul D. Meier, *Happiness is a Choice* (Grand Rapids, Mich.: Baker Book House, 1978), 174.

CHAPTER 3

1. Mels Carbonell, Ph.D., *Discover Your Giftedness in Christ, Combination Profile 3 Lessons Study Guide.* Copyright 1966 by Mels Carbonell, Ph.D.

CHAPTER 4

1. A. W. Tozer, *The Pursuit of God* (Fleming H. Revelle Co.: Old Tappan, N.J.: 1982), 126.
2. W. Glyn Evans, *Daily With the King* (Chicago, IL: Moody Press, 1979), 249.
3. Andrew Murray, cited in Warren and Ruth Myers, *31 Days of Prayer* (Sisters, OR.: Questar Publishers, Inc., 1997), 159.
4. Myers, 42.
5. V. Raymond Edman, *They Found the Secret* (Grand Rapids, MI: Zondervan, 1984), 19.

6. Myers, 158.
7. A.Wetherell Johnson, Bible Study Fellowship notes.

CHAPTER 5

1. *The Life Application Bible—The Living Bible* (Wheaton, Ill.: Tyndale House, 1988), 1934. [paraphrased]
2. Dr. James C. Dobson, *Straight Talk* (Dallas, London, Vancouver, Melbourne: Word Publishing, 1991), 100–1.
3. John F. Walvoord and Roy B. Zuck, *The Bible Knowledge Commentary* (Wheaton, Ill.: Victor Books, 1983), 683.

CHAPTER 6

1. 1 Peter 2 (AMP).
2. *New Webster's Dictionary and Thesaurus of the English Language* (Danbury, Conn.: Lexicon Publications, Inc., 1993), 848.
3. Ibid., 252.
4. Ibid., 851.
5. Ibid., 579.
6. Ibid., 58.
7. Ibid., 57.
8. Ibid., 923.
9. Ibid., 707.
10. Ibid., 413.

CHAPTER 7

1. *New Webster's Dictionary and Thesaurus of the English Language* (Danbury, Conn.: Lexicon Publications, Inc., 1993), 511.
2. Ibid., 581.

CHAPTER 9

1.  Lawrence J. Crabb, Jr., *The Marriage Builder* (Grand Rapids, Mich.: Zondervan Publishing House, 1982), 58–9.

CHAPTER 10

1.  Karen Burton Main, *Karen, Karen!* (Wheaton, Ill.: Tyndale House, 1979), 176.

EPILOGUE

1.  Charles R. Swindoll, *Strike the Original Match* (Portland, Ore.: Multnomah Press, 1980), 59.